A Digital Path to Sustainable Infrastructure Management

A Digital Path to Sustainable Infrastructure Management: Emerging Tools for the Construction Industry

BY

AYODEJI E. OKE
Federal University of Technology Akure, Nigeria

AND

SEYI S. STEPHEN
Federal University of Technology Akure, Nigeria

United Kingdom – North America – Japan – India – Malaysia – China

Emerald Publishing Limited
Emerald Publishing, Floor 5, Northspring, 21-23 Wellington Street, Leeds LS1 4DL

First edition 2024

British Library Cataloguing in Publication Data
A catalogue record for this book is available from the British Library

ISBN: 978-1-83797-704-8 (Print)
ISBN: 978-1-83797-703-1 (Online)
ISBN: 978-1-83797-705-5 (Epub)

INVESTOR IN PEOPLE

This book is dedicated to God who made all things beautiful.

Contents

List of Figures

About the Authors

Ayodeji E. Oke is an Author and a Lecturer with several years of teaching and research involvement in higher institutions of learning across the world. He founded the Research Group on Sustainable Infrastructure Management plus (RG-SIM+) and he is currently the leader of the team. He has over 350 publications including eight (8) books in the area of Sustainable Infrastructure Management (SIM) with focus on Sustainable Development, Digital Construction, Quantity Surveying, Value Management and other multidisciplinary research areas. He is currently a member of the Department of Quantity Surveying, Federal University of Technology Akure, Nigeria. He is also a Research Associate at University of Johannesburg, South Africa and an Academic Fellow at Universiti Sains Malaysia.

Seyi S. Stephen is a Construction Manager and a graduate of Federal University of Technology, Akure, Nigeria. He is a Social Psychology and Behavioural Sciences Enthusiast. He is a member of the Research Group on Sustainable Infrastructure Management plus (RG-SIM+) and he is currently a research coordinator. He also has a flair for literature and his areas of specialisation are academic consultancy, psychological education and teaching. He has authored books including *Sustainable Construction in Era of the Fourth Industrial Revolution published by Taylor and Francis*, Routledge, *Value Management Implementation in Construction* published by Emerald Publication and *Smart Cities: A Panacea for Sustainable Development published* by Emerald Publication.

Preface

The construction industry over the years has improved its activities from basic to advanced practices cutting across several construction stages (pre-construction, construction and post-construction). Through the implementation of several functional practices, the industry has been able to move towards construction that involves the application of digital advancements (construction 4.0) into enhancing project design, execution and management of developmental and infrastructural projects. With innovations in the current Fourth Industrial Revolution era (Industry 4.0 age) comes certain changes and deviations. It is, therefore, necessary to manage these differences in the best ways as the construction industry aims for the summit of project delivery with regards to traditional (cost, quality and duration) and emerging project delivery indices. There are several management practices already in place in construction such as risk management, value management, lean management and project management among others that are designed to cater for shortcomings that might occur in construction irrespective of the project phase as well as the method of execution. However, with constant changes in development and growth experienced in the construction industry as it works in line with meeting the incessant demands of the client, and considering modifications that come with management practices, especially with newly adopted technological advancements, it is important to consider how these practices will affect construction process and how these effects can be managed in this digital age.

Sustainable infrastructural management (SIM) is a concept that adopts sustainability principles in the design, construction and management of infrastructural projects using several sustainable practices and digital technologies. By inculcating these practices into construction stages, the industry is set to maximise potential in terms of benefits that come with the application of digital technologies in project delivery. While not neglecting challenges, barriers and other related peculiarities about their functionalities, this book is designed to assist the readers with general oversight of the gap these technologies and practices can fill in terms of additions to both the stakeholders and the clients. Since this book is designed for comprehensiveness, it starts with a general introduction to the chapters and contents therein. Filling the knowledge gap in terms of processes, applications and executions, the chapters explain succinctly the relationship between the adoption of sustainable practices and construction in the digital age.

This book 'A Digital Path to Sustainable Infrastructure Management' explained the usage of digital tools and technologies such as connected machines, grid computing, mobile cloud computing, smart contract, quantum computing, smart computing, cognitive radio, cyber technology, Radio Frequency Identification (RFID), mechatronics and digital twins for delivery of construction and developmental projects. This book can be used as a research framework by professionals in the architecture, engineering, construction and operation (AECO) industries. With no limitations, the expected readers of this book include construction and engineering professionals in various fields; undergraduate and postgraduate students in the construction and built environment-related disciplines; stakeholders and policymakers in the architecture, engineering, construction and operation (AECO) industry; urban and regional planners; procurement officers in ministries (private and public); construction workers/enthusiasts in both developing and developed countries; building, civil and industrial stakeholders; project managers; value creators across several fields; individuals concerned with building a smart and sustainable city; and building contractors and regulatory project personnel amongst other readers.

Ayodeji E. Oke
Seyi S. Stephen

Part I
General Introduction of the Book

Chapter 1

General Introduction

Abstract

In terms of having the general idea of what the whole book entails, the first chapter gave an insight into all the chapters and what details each chapter holds. This chapter began with an introduction of the book title in relation to the construction industry and sustainable practice in a collaborative manner. In addition, sustainable infrastructure management (SIM) was discussed in relation to construction Industry 4.0 and the management qualities of the technologies incorporated into construction activities. The objective of the book gave the need for SIM in construction with the view of achieving sustainable practices beneficial to both the client and the construction professional.

Keywords: Construction management; digital construction; project delivery; standard construction; sustainable construction; sustainable infrastructure

Introduction

The construction industry has improved its activities over the years to cater to the demands of the clients. Not only are the demands met presently, but construction professionals have also been working towards making provisions for the future through several sustainable practices. Sustainable construction is that which encompasses the implementation of modern technologies into construction from the onset of project planning through completion and finally into management.

The concept of sustainable construction has gained more recognition across construction industries. Even though the practice is more common among the developed countries of the world, developing countries are also not left behind. Through a gradual process, sustainable construction has been introduced and somewhat practiced concerning the region, culture, feasibility and capacity of the construction professionals present in the countries. With sustainability taking centre stage in advanced construction, there is a need to discuss more functionalities of sustainable practices regarding its benefits, challenges, management and its interactions within the internal and external environments of the construction process. These

A Digital Path to Sustainable Infrastructure Management, 3–14

Copyright © 2024 Ayodeji E. Oke and Seyi S. Stephen

Published under exclusive licence by Emerald Publishing Limited

doi:10.1108/978-1-83797-703-120241001

factors determine the way it relates to construction and how sustainable practices can be maximised to obtain the desired results it was formulated for in the first place.

This book is divided into two parts. The first details the general introduction of the book while the second part details other chapters related to sustainable infrastructure management (SIM) in the digital age. The first chapter that makes the first part of the book gives a general introduction to what the book entails, the objective of the book, and other related topics about sustainable development in construction. Since it is a research book, the abstract is provided as well as the conclusion to give the reader a summary of the chapter. Chapter 2 of the book, digital transformation was introduced along with its drivers, benefits, challenges and its applications in construction. Chapter 3, digital technologies further discussed the applications of these digital technologies in sustainable construction activities along with benefits, challenges and drivers which one way or the other affects its implementation into construction across different phases of project execution. The next two, chapters 4 and 5 discussed connected machines and ecological economics. Along with the introductions on what the topics entail, their involvement in sustainable construction was explained. Also, other sections like challenges, drivers, benefits and other sub-topics were annotated to give the topics an expected knowledge contribution to the readers. Chapter 6 is about grid computing in today's construction, how it works in construction activities, drivers, challenges and its characteristics towards construction in terms of application and functionalities.

Mobile cloud computing is the seventh chapter discussed in construction along with its benefits in construction management. Its mitigations in adopting the practice were also highlighted and further concluded. Chapter 8 is a smart contract introduced into construction through blockchain. Its application in today's world, different types, challenges as well as its benefits when incorporated into construction contracts. With further studies on smart contracts, chapter 9 in quantum computing discusses new trends in construction. Some of the trends include smart contracts, construction drones, augmented reality (AR), etc. Also, the evolution of quantum computing in architecture, details of quantum computing, drivers, applications and challenges make up the entire chapter. Chapter 10, smart computing shows how the system works in construction management, its supporting programmes and applications using business intelligence, coupled with its benefits and challenges. The next chapter, cognitive radio in construction highlights spectrum sensing techniques, their applications in today's construction and challenges. Chapter 12 is for radio frequency identification. Its usefulness in construction projects, along with its realities and benefits are discussed in the aim to manage construction as it further moves towards sustainability. The concluding chapters in cyber technology, mechatronics and digital twins centred on digitalisation in construction, various drivers, challenges and benefits, applications in construction projects, how they are influencing modern construction, and so on.

Sustainable Infrastructure Management (SIM)

SIM in construction refers to the process of planning, designing, constructing, operating and maintaining infrastructure in a way that minimises negative environmental impacts, optimises resource efficiency and promotes long-term social and economic benefits.

SIM is the incorporation of sustainable practices (technologies) into construction. Thorough the application of several technologies, the construction industry has advanced progressively in terms of output, quality and delivery over the years. In Oke, Aigbavboa, Stephen, and Thwala (2021), the following technologies were discussed in relation towards engaging digital construction (Construction 4.0) into project enhancement, delivery and management. These technologies include:

- Artificial intelligence (AI),
- Augmented reality (AR),
- Big data,
- Building Information Modelling (BIM),
- Biomimicry,
- Blockchain,
- Cryptocurrency,
- Cyber security,
- Drone,
- Gamification,
- Internet of Things (IoT),
- Machine learning (ML),
- Nanotechnology,
- Robotics, and
- Virtual reality (VR).

These technologies were discussed to provide the influence of sustainable practices in the Fourth Industrial Revolution in the construction industry. However, the introduction and implementation of practices such as digital transformation, digital technologies, connected machines, ecological economics, grid computing, mobile cloud computing, smart contract, quantum computing, smart computing, cognitive radio, radio frequency identification, cyber technology, mechatronics and digital twins in construction are set to do more than bring out benefits of sustainable practices but also help in managing infrastructures now and in the future context. Inculcating these practices as management platforms will propel the construction industry more towards sustainability and functionality without having to worry about providing alternatives as regards when traditional construction practices are used in construction.

Sustainable Design and Planning

Effective SIM starts with the design and planning phase. This involves going beyond traditional approaches and incorporating sustainable design principles. Green building practices, such as energy-efficient design, passive cooling strategies, use of renewable materials and consideration of life-cycle assessments, are integrated into the design process. By optimising energy performance, minimising resource consumption and reducing environmental impact from the start, sustainable design and planning lay the foundation for sustainable infrastructure projects.

Energy Efficiency Measures

Energy consumption in infrastructure is a significant contributor to environmental impact. Implementing energy-efficient measures is essential for SIM. This includes utilising renewable energy sources like solar or wind power, optimising lighting systems with energy-saving technologies such as LED, and adopting smart grid technologies for efficient energy distribution. By reducing energy demand and reliance on fossil fuels, these measures help decrease greenhouse gas emissions and enhance the overall sustainability of infrastructure projects.

Water Management Strategies

Water scarcity and the need for sustainable water use are growing concerns globally. SIM incorporates water management strategies to ensure responsible water usage in construction projects. This includes techniques like rainwater harvesting, which collects and stores rainwater for various non-potable uses, such as irrigation or toilet flushing. Wastewater recycling systems can treat and reuse water, minimising the strain on freshwater resources. Additionally, implementing efficient irrigation systems with water-saving technologies helps reduce water consumption and promotes sustainable water management practices.

Materials Selection and Waste Management

SIM prioritises the use of eco-friendly and locally sourced materials. This involves selecting materials with a lower environmental footprint, such as recycled or renewable materials, and reducing reliance on materials associated with high carbon emissions or environmental damage. Additionally, waste management practices play a crucial role in sustainable infrastructure. Adopting strategies like construction waste recycling, where materials are sorted, processed and reused, helps minimise the amount of waste sent to landfills. By reducing waste generation and promoting circular economy principles, SIM contributes to a more sustainable construction industry.

Green Transportation and Mobility

Transportation is a significant contributor to air pollution, congestion and carbon emissions. SIM recognises the importance of promoting green transportation options and integrating sustainable mobility solutions. This includes designing infrastructure that prioritises walking and cycling by incorporating pedestrian-friendly pathways, dedicated bike lanes and bike-sharing systems. It also involves creating efficient and accessible public transit networks that encourage public transportation usage, reducing reliance on private vehicles. By prioritising sustainable transportation, infrastructure management helps reduce traffic congestion, improve air quality and lower carbon emissions.

Resilience and Climate Change Adaptation

Climate change poses significant challenges to infrastructure systems, making resilience and adaptation essential in SIM. Infrastructure projects must consider the potential impacts of climate change, such as increased frequency of extreme weather events, sea-level rise and changing precipitation patterns. SIM incorporates climate-resilient design features like flood-resistant structures, sustainable drainage systems and nature-based solutions that enhance infrastructure resilience. By building resilient infrastructure that can withstand and adapt to climate change impacts, SIM ensures long-term functionality and reduces vulnerability to climate-related risks.

Stakeholder Engagement and Social Considerations

SIM prioritises stakeholder engagement and social equity. It recognises the importance of including local communities, affected stakeholders and marginalised groups in the decision-making processes. Engaging stakeholders from the early stages of project development, listening to their concerns and incorporating their feedback helps build trust and ensures that infrastructure projects meet the needs of the community. Furthermore, social considerations are integrated into infrastructure management, addressing social needs, promoting inclusivity and considering the socio-economic impacts of projects. By fostering social equity and community involvement, SIM contributes to sustainable and inclusive development.

Monitoring and Performance Evaluation

Monitoring and performance evaluation are crucial components of SIM. Implementing monitoring systems allows for the measurement and assessment of key sustainability indicators such as energy consumption, water usage, waste generation and environmental impacts. By continuously monitoring infrastructure performance, managers can identify areas for improvement, track progress towards sustainability goals and make data-driven decisions. Regular performance evaluation enables optimisation of resource utilisation, identification of inefficiencies and the implementation of corrective measures to enhance the overall sustainability and effectiveness of infrastructure projects.

Innovative Technologies and Future Trends

Embracing innovative technologies and staying informed about future trends is essential for SIM. Technologies like BIM, IoT, AI and data analytics offer significant opportunities for enhancing sustainable infrastructure practices. BIM allows for better project visualisation, collaboration and optimisation of resources. IoT sensors enable real-time monitoring of infrastructure systems, enabling predictive maintenance and efficient resource management. AI and data analytics provide insights for improving energy efficiency, optimising traffic flow and making informed decisions. By incorporating these innovative technologies, SIM can drive efficiency, enhance resilience and foster continuous improvement.

Collaboration and Knowledge Sharing

Collaboration and knowledge sharing are fundamental for SIM. Infrastructure projects involve various stakeholders, including government agencies, private companies, academia and communities. Collaborative partnerships allow for the exchange of expertise, experiences and best practices. Sharing knowledge and lessons learnt from successful sustainable infrastructure projects helps create a collective learning environment. Collaboration also enables the pooling of resources, funding opportunities and the development of innovative solutions. By fostering collaboration and knowledge sharing, SIM can benefit from collective wisdom, avoid duplicating efforts and accelerate the transition towards a more sustainable and resilient infrastructure sector.

Concept of SIM

SIM encompasses the holistic approach of planning, designing, constructing, operating and maintaining infrastructure systems while considering economic, environmental and social sustainability factors.

Environmental Considerations

This explores the environmental aspects of SIM, including reducing greenhouse gas emissions, minimising resource consumption, protecting biodiversity and addressing climate change resilience.

Economic Viability

Examining the economic dimension, this subsection focuses on cost-effectiveness, life cycle costing and long-term financial sustainability of infrastructure projects, considering factors like initial investment, maintenance costs and potential economic benefits.

Social Equity and Community Engagement

Here, the importance of ensuring social equity, inclusiveness and community engagement in infrastructure planning and decision-making processes is emphasised, highlighting the need to address social needs, promote accessibility and consider the social impact on local communities.

Policy and Governance

This section explores the role of policy frameworks, regulations and governance structures in promoting SIM. It discusses the importance of integrating sustainability principles into policies, establishing clear guidelines and fostering collaboration between stakeholders.

Resilience and Risk Management

Examining the concept of resilience, this subsection emphasises the need to assess and manage risks associated with infrastructure systems, considering potential natural disasters, climate change impacts and other uncertainties to ensure the long-term functionality and adaptability of infrastructure.

Innovation and Technology

Here, the role of innovation and technology in SIM is discussed. This includes exploring digital tools, smart technologies and data-driven approaches that enhance efficiency, optimise resource utilisation and enable real-time monitoring and decision-making.

Sustainable Construction Practices

This section focuses on sustainable construction techniques, such as green building materials, energy-efficient designs, construction waste management and adopting environmentally friendly construction practices to minimise environmental impacts during the construction phase.

Performance Monitoring and Evaluation

Highlighting the significance of monitoring and evaluating infrastructure performance, this subsection emphasises the use of indicators, metrics and data analysis to track the effectiveness of sustainability strategies, identify areas for improvement and support evidence-based decision-making.

Collaboration and Partnerships

This underscores the importance of collaboration and partnerships among various stakeholders, including government entities, private sectors, academia and civil society, to foster knowledge sharing, innovation and collective action towards SIM.

Challenges of SIM

The challenges below underscore the need for proactive and holistic approaches to SIM, where innovative solutions, policy reforms, stakeholder engagement and long-term planning are combined to overcome obstacles and achieve sustainable development objectives.

Complexity of Interconnected Systems

Managing sustainable infrastructure involves dealing with interconnected systems such as transportation, energy, water and waste. Coordinating and integrating these systems pose challenges due to their complexity, requiring multidisciplinary approaches and collaboration between various stakeholders.

Financing and Funding

Sustainable infrastructure projects often require significant upfront investments, making financing and funding a major challenge. Securing long-term funding sources and incentivising private sector participation in sustainable infrastructure development are critical challenges that need to be addressed.

Policy and Regulatory Barriers

Inconsistent or inadequate policies and regulations can hinder the implementation of sustainable infrastructure practices. Addressing regulatory barriers, streamlining permitting processes and providing supportive policy frameworks are essential to foster sustainable infrastructure development.

Technological Advancements and Innovation

Adopting new technologies and innovative solutions is crucial for SIM. However, keeping up with rapidly evolving technologies, their integration into existing systems and managing the potential risks associated with their implementation pose challenges that need to be overcome.

Knowledge and Capacity Gaps

Building a skilled workforce and promoting knowledge exchange are challenges in SIM. Enhancing capacity building initiatives, providing training programmes and fostering knowledge-sharing platforms can help address these gaps.

Stakeholder Engagement and Collaboration

Engaging diverse stakeholders and fostering collaboration among them is essential for successful SIM. However, managing conflicting interests, ensuring effective participation and maintaining consistent communication pose challenges that need to be navigated.

Balancing Economic and Environmental Objectives

SIM requires striking a balance between economic development and environmental conservation. Balancing these objectives can be challenging, as economic considerations often take precedence, making it crucial to integrate sustainability into the decision-making process.

Resilience and Climate Change Adaptation

Climate change poses significant challenges to infrastructure management. Ensuring infrastructure resilience and adapting to climate change impacts, such as sea-level rise, extreme weather events and changing precipitation patterns, require proactive planning, risk assessments and investments in resilient design.

Existing Infrastructure Retrofitting

Addressing the sustainability of existing infrastructure is a challenge. Retrofitting and upgrading existing infrastructure to meet sustainability standards can be complex, costly and disruptive. Developing strategies for retrofitting and repurposing infrastructure assets is crucial for SIM.

Long-Term Planning and Decision-Making

Infrastructure projects have long lifecycles, and decisions made during the planning phase have long-lasting impacts. The challenge lies in integrating sustainability considerations into long-term planning and decision-making processes, ensuring that projects align with sustainable development goals and future needs.

Need for SIM

As identified in the study by Oke, Stephen, Aigbavboa, Ogunsemi, and Aje (2022), the construction industry needs to do better in the application of digital technologies into construction activities. Since buildings are getting more complex, coupled with the high demand of the client in line with green standard, working towards SIM practices will aid construction professionals in terms of:

- Project delivery,
- Cost maximisation,
- Project enhancement,
- Construction management,
- Sustainable construction,
- Project quality,
- Monitoring and performance, etc.

Environmental Conservation

SIM is essential for environmental conservation. By integrating environmentally friendly practices, such as minimising carbon emissions, reducing resource consumption and protecting natural habitats, it helps mitigate the negative impacts of infrastructure on ecosystems and contributes to the preservation of biodiversity.

Climate Change Mitigation and Adaptation

Addressing climate change is a pressing need in infrastructure management. Sustainable infrastructure practices, including the use of renewable energy sources, promoting energy efficiency and implementing climate-resilient designs, help mitigate greenhouse gas emissions and enhance infrastructure's resilience to climate change impacts.

Resource Efficiency

SIM focuses on optimising resource utilisation. By adopting efficient technologies, materials and processes, it reduces resource consumption, minimises waste generation and promotes the circular economy, ensuring the long-term availability of resources for future generations.

Social Equity and Inclusivity

Promoting social equity and inclusivity is a critical need in infrastructure management. Sustainable infrastructure should prioritise accessibility, accommodate diverse user needs and consider the social impact on local communities. It helps create inclusive spaces, improve quality of life and reduce social inequalities.

Economic Development and Job Creation

Sustainable infrastructure can be a catalyst for economic development and job creation. By investing in sustainable infrastructure projects, countries can stimulate economic growth, create employment opportunities and enhance productivity, contributing to long-term socio-economic prosperity.

Public Health and Safety

SIM plays a vital role in ensuring public health and safety. By implementing measures such as improved sanitation systems, safe drinking water supply and disaster-resilient infrastructure, it protects public health and reduces the vulnerability of communities to hazards.

Long-Term Cost Savings

Investing in sustainable infrastructure can yield long-term cost savings. Although sustainable infrastructure projects may require higher upfront investments, they often result in reduced operational and maintenance costs over their lifecycle. Energy-efficient designs, for example, can lead to significant savings in energy consumption and operational expenses.

Urbanisation and Population Growth

With rapid urbanisation and population growth, the need for SIM becomes even more critical. By providing efficient transportation systems, affordable housing and well-designed public spaces, sustainable infrastructure helps address the challenges associated with urbanisation and promotes livable cities.

Technological Advancements and Innovation

The integration of technological advancements and innovation is essential in SIM. Embracing smart technologies, data analytics and digital solutions can optimise resource allocation, enhance operational efficiency and enable real-time monitoring, leading to more sustainable and resilient infrastructure systems.

International Commitments and Sustainability Goals

The fulfilment of international commitments and sustainability goals necessitates SIM. Initiatives such as the United Nations Sustainable Development Goals (SDGs) and the Paris Agreement on climate change call for the implementation of sustainable infrastructure to achieve global targets and ensure a sustainable future for all.

These needs emphasise the importance of adopting SIM practices to address environmental, social and economic challenges, create resilient communities and work towards a more sustainable and inclusive future.

Objective of the Book

Several researchers have worked on acclimatising sustainable practices in construction, as well as inculcating various management practices into construction activities in order to arrive at a set output, out of which are presented in studies by Isa, Jimoh, and Achuenu (2013), Agarwal, Chandrasekaran, and Sridhar (2016), Zhan, Pan, Javed, and Chau (2018), Ghodoosi, Bagchi, Hosseini, Vilutien, and Zeynalian (2021), Fathalizadeh et al. (2021), Oke et al. (2021, 2022) among others.

This book is written to identify and merge functionalities of digital technologies activities in construction along with management potentials towards sustainable construction. Also, the book is designed to help construction professionals, stakeholders, scholars and concerned individuals regarding the concept of sustainable construction for project planning, execution, management and enhancement for improved construction practice.

References

Agarwal, R., Chandrasekaran, S., & Sridhar, M. (2016). *Imagining construction's digital future.* Retrieved from https://www.mckinsey.com

Fathalizadeh, A., Hosseini, M. R., Vaezzadeh, S. S., Edwards, D. J., Martek, I., & Shooshtarian, S. (2021). Barriers to sustainable construction project management: The case of Iran. *Smart and Sustainable Built Environment, 2*(1), 1–24. doi:10.1108/SASBE-09-2020-0132

Ghodoosi, F., Bagchi, A., Hosseini, M. R., Vilutien, E. T., & Zeynalian, M. (2021). Enhancement of bid decision-making in construction projects: A reliability analysis approach. *Journal of Civil Engineering and Management, 27*(2), 149–161.

Isa, R. B., Jimoh, R. A., & Achuenu, E. (2013). An overview of the contribution of construction sector to sustainable development in Nigeria. *Net Journal of Business Management, 1*(1), 1–6.

Oke, A. E., Aigbavboa, C. O., Stephen, S. S., & Thwala, W. D. (2021). *Sustainable construction in the era of the fourth industrial revolution.* London and New York, NY: Taylor and Francis Group. doi:10.1201/9781003179849-1

Oke, A. E., Stephen, S. S., Aigbavboa, C. O., Ogunsemi, D. R., & Aje, I. O. (2022). *Smart cities: A panacea for sustainable construction.* Bingley: Emerald Publishing Limited.

Zhan, W., Pan, W., Javed, A. A., & Chau, K. W. (2018). Correlation analysis of key influencing factors to the total factor productivity of the Hong Kong construction industry. In *Proceedings of the 21st International Symposium on Advancement of Construction Management and Real Estate,* January 6–8, China. doi:10.1007/978-981-10-6190-5_51

Part II
Digital Tools and Sustainable Infrastructure Management

Chapter 2

Digital Transformation for Sustainable Infrastructure Management

Abstract

Digital transformation is essential for the development of the construction sector with the opportunities it offers to change and optimise the construction business. Digitalisation affects every stage and process, the whole value chain. As for some other industries, as well as in the construction sector, it provides several advantages and benefits which include increased productivity; increased speed of construction and saving time in the implementation of construction projects, significantly higher quality of accompanying construction documentation, etc. At the same time, there are some challenges related to the lag of digital transformation in construction when compared to other sectors. Some of these challenges are in the presence of some specific technical challenges, different degrees of application of new information technology in smaller construction companies, and so on which are often in the role of subcontractors and other parties involved in construction implementation. Despite the challenges, digital transformation has no alternative given the future upward development of the construction sector as the industry drives towards sustainability.

Keywords: Construction economy; construction management; digital construction; digital transformation; project transformation; sustainable construction

Introduction

The 'construction sector' is of key importance to the development of the world's economy. It accounts for 6% of the global gross domestic product (GDP) (World Economic Forum, 2017). Construction is associated with almost all other industries. For other industries to function, they usually rely on buildings or assets that have to be built. In addition, it should be noted that constructed assets, with all its diversities (residential buildings, roads, bridges, schools, hospitals, etc.),

A Digital Path to Sustainable Infrastructure Management, 17–25
Copyright © 2024 Ayodeji E. Oke and Seyi S. Stephen
Published under exclusive licence by Emerald Publishing Limited
doi:10.1108/978-1-83797-703-120241002

have direct impacts on the quality of life of the people. Furthermore, the prospects of intensive development of the construction sector in the future are related to rapid urbanisation and investment in digital practices. As an example of the expected prospects can be pointed in the assessment of the growth of urban populated areas with an increase of about 200,000 people a day. In this connection, it should be in mind that the residents of these areas will need housing, transportation, communal and other infrastructural developments and this are all connected to the construction industry somehow (World Economic Forum, 2017).

Digital transformation brings about a paradigm shift from traditional construction to a more technological advanced practices. These are practices infused into construction through different construction rerated practices especially in the era of the fourth industrial revolution (Construction 4.0). With advancements somewhat implemented in some developed countries in the fifth industrial revolution through the adoption of further technological systems in internet of everything (IoE), smart cities, smart computation, etc., the construction sector is deemed to reach newer summits when these practices are fully operational (Oke, Aigbavboa, Stephen, & Thwala, 2021).

Digitalisation in Construction

The construction industry according to Isa, Jimoh, and Achuenu (2013) may be viewed as that sector of the economy which, through planning, design, construction, maintenance and repair and operation, transforms various resources into constructed facilities. It is a sector of the economy that transforms various resources into constructed physical, economic and social infrastructure necessary for socioeconomic development (Ezeokoli, Ugochukwu, Agu, & Akabougu, 2016). The industry contributes significantly to the GDP of any nation. In Nigeria for instance, the industry contributed about 4.13% to the total real GDP in the first quarter of 2016 (National Bureau of Statistics [NBS, 2022]). Also, around the world, the industry has fared well both in job creation and the socioeconomic development of the nations.

The industry just like every other sector is facing a paradigm shift as new technologies otherwise referred to as disruptive technology is gathering momentum in the world. The driving forces in the construction industry indicate that the ability to innovate is quickly becoming a competitive necessity (Tatum, 1989). Bossink (2004) agreed that driving innovation on the trans-firm, intra-firm and inter-firm level in the network of organisations is an opportunity for managers of both public and private organisations to develop, improve and renew their organisations' positions in the market, the quality of their organisation's projects and the cooperative structure of the industry as a whole. Stressing this emphasis, Bahl (2015) argued that no industry is immune to the impact of digital disruption, even the highly-regulated industries, such as financial services, are under intense pressure to recast their operations. Also, this wave of disruption is not just for companies; society is also feeling the heat of transformation towards a better future that is digitally driven (Capgemini Consulting, 2013). Hence, technologies are changing businesses today and are making clients/consumers break the norms of business such that every business requires a digital orientation, meaning a digital focus in all business processes and functions (Brea-Solís, Casadesus-Masanell, & Grifell-Tatjé, 2014). However, Ezeokoli, Ugochukwu, et al. (2016) observed that the construction and real estate sector, for example, ranks lowest in terms of digital maturity, that is, the industry is lagging behind other industries that use information communication and technology (ICT). So, to avoid being left out of the competition, the construction industry needs to change its modus operandi to that befitting and beneficial to this digital-driven era. This needs to happen rapidly because most clients and consumers are getting more informed now and about 40% of the world population today are digitally compliance; those that cannot keep up with pace may be running the risk of being pushed out of business by competitors that are responding rapidly in the direction of digital advancement (Corver & Elkhuizen, 2014).

In becoming a digital enterprise, the construction industry will be required to thoroughly reimage the industry through the digital lens in terms of its processes and customer engagement (Brea-Solís et al., 2014). Also, it will have to develop further digital strategies with more defined scopes and objectives on how to achieve and stay relevant during the incessant digital transformation. This is because the ultimate power of a digital strategy lies in its scope and objectives as saliently highlighted by Corver and Elkhuizen (2014). It is therefore important to note that the evolving nature of technology makes transformation not a one-time investment and initiative; but the organisational, operational and technological foundations are put in place to foster constant evolution and cross-functional collaboration (Ernest & Young, 2015). To make this work, the strategies to be further developed should be such that they will win the hearts and minds of people at all levels in the organisation (Capgemini Consulting, 2013). When the industry is fully digitalised, clients' demands and expectations, as well as the obligations of the contractors are met within stipulated project duration, quality and cost (Corver & Elkhuizen, 2014).

Drivers of Digital Transformation Application in Construction

Drivers for digital transformation are proving pivotal to how the construction sector competes, innovates and adopts practices intending to enhance customer satisfaction (Shah, Hartman, & Whimmple, 2014). Accordingly, the proliferation of digital channels, platforms and devices has helped to accelerate the emergence of a new digital world, and its impacts are impossible to ignore (Ernest & Young, 2015).

Drivers

Several studies in Bahl (2015); International Data Group (IDG) (2012) and Capgemini Consulting (2013) have articulated key drivers to digital transformation for any business, they include:

- Growth in new revenue and profitability,
- Satisfaction of the customer within affordable prices,

- Increased production and operation efficiencies in every aspect of goods and services,
- Enhanced market strategic flexibility,
- Improved employees welfare,
- Vast knowledge of the market condition, and
- Efficient data storage and management.

Benefits of Digital Transformation for Construction Project

Digital transformation is essential for the development of the construction sector with the opportunities it offers to change and optimise the construction business. Digital transformation affects every stage of it, its processes and the whole value chain. As for many other industries, as well as in the construction sector, it has many advantages. The following benefits are indicated below in the study by Aghimien, Aigbavboa, Oke and Koloko (2018):

- Enhancement in production and delivery,
- Project delivery within contract budget and duration,
- Smooth running of construction activities in respect to the programme of work designed,
- Improved standard and specification in regards project details,
- Enhanced building designs through quality assessment, etc.

Other benefits may include:

- Propel sustainable development of projects,
- Facilitate value development and management,
- Enhanced construction estimation towards project whole life cycle,
- Improved relationship between the client and the construction professionals,
- Identification of challenges pre, during, after construction,
- Through improved project delivery and the economy,
- Enablement of sustainable practices towards project enhancement, etc.

Research shows that despite the situation whereby the construction industry lags in swift digital transformation adoption, the ones implemented have benefited the industry in massive ways. Also, the construction sector growing rapidly and thus expanding the built industry to a more compound one, even though this growth cannot be compared with that of other industries in the economy. To illustrate this fact, Berger (2016) gave an example of construction productivity in Germany, which has grown by 4.1% over the last 10 years; while in the whole German economy, it has increased by 11% over the same period. The digitalisation in construction contributes to the reduction in construction costs along with the platform to deliver more successful projects within time and means.

Application and Technological Solution of Digital Transformation in the Construction Sector

In the field of construction, certain technological solutions and approaches in the field of information and communication technologies and digitalisation can be mentioned. These technologies influence the business practices of companies in the construction sector in a very favourable way, and thus give them many advantages as illustrated by Berger (2016) below:

- Use of digital platforms for the supply of raw materials:

As a rule, 'raw materials represent a substantial part of the total cost in the construction sector, and digital platforms contribute to reducing these costs'. According to statistics, electronic supply of raw materials helps *save, for example, 5% of the value of catalogue-based purchases* and *10% of value when auctioned*.

- Implementation of digital tools for smart logistics and maintenance of construction sites software for managing supply activities, exploiting the capabilities of the internet of things (IoT) and radio frequency identification technologies:

In construction, the following specifics are observed – construction workers use only about 30% of their working time to carry out their main activity. The remaining 70% is used for supplementary activities such as transporting materials, cleaning, rearranging the construction site, searching for materials and equipment, etc. This ratio in the use of working time can be optimised with the help of digital tools, with which the benefits of digitalisation are widespread. Such digital assets could function in the use of supply management software, which results in materials being shipped to the construction site at the exact time when they are needed; while work on storage and rearrangement on the sites can be minimised to the lowest possibility.

Another 'possibility of intelligent logistics is the *intelligent, connected construction machines* as part of the work environment in the context of the IoT. These machines can have appropriate *sensors*, which can optimize the work of construction workers and their auxiliary equipment (hoists and vehicles, etc.) – less waste of time for coordination and efficiency by synchronizing the base sensor signals, which can be seen as an undoubted advantage as a result of digital' transformation.

Radio Frequency Identification (RFID) technology is also an important digital tool. Building materials, equipment and products, equipped with this technology can be identified and tracked by electromagnetic fields. They can be recorded and scanned, thus optimising their location on the construction site.

- Use of drones, robots and 3D technology:

The use of drones in the construction industry can potentially be useful at various stages of construction projects – in the preliminary planning, detailed exploration and mapping of the construction site, monitoring of the construction process, post-construction inspections, sales and marketing (Anwar, Izhar, & Najam, 2018). Drones can have a variety of equipment, such as a high-resolution camera, 3D capture and video streaming, RFID reader, global positioning system (GPS) device, Wi-Fi communication and more. The data obtained from the sensors of these unmanned aerial vehicles can be processed and analysed to provide important business information. Drones can be applied at every stage of the construction from pre-construction and throughout other construction phases by providing information from/for the site of designers, construction contractors and construction supervisors in terms of processes, challenges, priorities, etc. even to the final stages of the construction project especially when preparing impact assessment reports. Subsequently, intelligent monitoring of the construction process can significantly reduce the effort and cost of monitoring and reporting construction procedures, which are particularly large when implemented traditionally, especially in large-scale construction sites. Other benefits include cost saving, construction precision, and enhanced project delivery tailored towards improving project performance across every phase of planning, construction and management.

In addition, robots can bring significant benefits to the efficiency and pro-ductivity of construction work. They are used for mapping the construction site, laying bricks, preparing the necessary materials, etc. (Jayaraj & Divakar, 2018). Robots can replace humans in construction activities, such as working with chemical dyes, at high altitudes and lots more especially in areas that pose a threat to normal working conditions. Specific construction practices which require several weeks of normal construction activity are carried out within reduced duration with the help of a robot using 3D construction technologies (Berger, 2016). The benefits of implementing this technology are also cost saving, con-struction precision, enhanced project delivery tailored towards improved project performance across every phase of planning, construction and management.

Challenges of Digital Transformation for Construction Project

The implementation of 'digitalisation and digital transformation' in the con-struction sector can be associated with some challenges that need to be taken into account. In its study, the McKinsey Research Company (McKinsey, 2016) found a lag in the construction sector in terms of its degree of digitalisation based on its 2015 McKinsey Global Institute industry digitisation index among 22 compared sectors. Construction ranks second to last (after only the Agriculture and Hunting sectors). It can thus be said that the construction sector has not yet fully embraced new digital technologies that needed initial investment, even though the long-term benefits are considerably high. Also, expenditures on research and development in construction are far behind those in other industries; they represent less than 1% of revenue, while the benchmarks in automotive and aerospace sectors are between 3.5% and 4.5% respectively. For its part, information technology (IT) costs are also insufficient and account for less than 1% of construction revenues. The researcher further identifies technical challenges specific to the construction sector as one of the major causes of the slow pace of digitalisation. The varying degrees of application of new IT in smaller construction companies, which are often played by the role of subcontractors, may also be challenging towards fully implementing digital technologies in construction.

In a further study by Berger (2016), several key points that are directly related to the ability to unleash the potential of digitalisation – digital data, digital access, automation and connectivity were identified. These key points can have impacts and become links in the value chain in the construction sector: in logistics, in the supply of raw materials, production and in production, marketing and sales and after-sales marketing. Firms in the construction sector face the challenge of deciding which approach to target and how to best implement it. Berger (2016) continued by pointing out that companies in the construction industry that are more focused on technological development and carefully consider how to apply technological innovations in the value chain are more likely to outperform competitive players because with the introduction of digital methods, they will become more productive and efficient.

Other researchers and research companies (Brea-Solís et al., 2014; Capgemini Consulting, 2013; Ezeokoli, Okolie, Okoye, & Belonwu, 2016) argue that firms need to face the multiple challenges of digital transformation to create a complete digital consumer experience, in order to meet expectations with every possible interaction. The major challenges inferred include from the studies are:

- Availability of capable team to manage digitally enabled project activities,
- Perception of some companies about the general idea of digitalisation in construction activities,
- Finding a balance in work, motivation and 'digital enthusiasm' between middle and operational levels staffs,
- Inadequate technical digital skills and expertise,
- Cost in upgrading from traditional to technological practices (training, workshop, exercise, etc.),
- The need to constantly improve (upgrade) digital services,
- Size of the firm,
- Nature of the project embarked upon, and
- Digital services are subject to hack hence loss of data and privacy.

Conclusion

This chapter identified the main benefits that digitalisation brings to the construction sector as it relates to increased productivity and efficiency, increased speed of construction activities, shortening the deadlines for implementation of construction projects and adhering to construction schedules, improved design of buildings, etc. On the other hand, findings across publications indicated the major challenges associated with the digitalisation of the construction industry include lag experienced in terms of its degree of digitalisation, some technical challenges, identifying the right resources needed for digitalisation, as well as adequately managing the right teams to accomplish digital transformation and so on. Companies in the construction sector are aware of the potential of emerging technologies such as building information modelling (BIM), 3D printing, robots, wireless sensing and other automated technologies, but they are not fully aware of exactly how to implement them in their organisations' strategy to enjoy the benefits that come with digitalisation in the construction industry. There are difficulties in identifying the right resources needed for digitalisation, as well as adequate management of the right digital transformation teams.

References

Aghimien, D., Aigbavboa, C., Oke, A., & Koloko, N. (2018). Digitalisation in construction industry. Construction professionals perspective. In *Proceeding of the Fourth Australiasia and South-East Asia Structural Engineering and Construction Conference*. Brisbane, Australia. 3–5. doi:10.14455ISEC.res.2018.90

Anwar, N., Izhar, M. A., & Najam, F. A. (2018). Construction monitoring and reporting using drones and unmanned aerial vehicles (UAVs). In *The Tenth International Conference on Construction in the 21st Century (CITC-10)*, July 2–4, Colombo, Sri Lanka.

Bahl, M. (2015). *Asia rising: Digital driving, cognizant centre for the future of work.* Retrieved from http://www.futureofwork.com

Berger, R. (2016). *Digitization in the construction industry, think act.* Retrieved from https://www.bergerholding.eu

Bossink, B. A. (2004). Managing drivers of innovation in construction networks. *Journal of Construction Engineering and Management, 130*(3), 337–345.

Brea-Solís, H., Casadesus-Masanell, R., & Grifell-Tatjé, E. (2014). Business model evaluation: Quantifying Walmart's sources of advantage. *Strategic Entrepreneurship Journal, 8*(4), 230–252.

Capgemini Consulting. (2013). *Accelerating digital transformation, digital transformation review.* Retrieved from https://www.slideshare.net

Corver, Q., & Elkhuizen, Q. (2014). *A framework for digital business transformation.* Cognizant. Retrieved from http://www.cognizant.com

Ernest, E., & Young, Y. (2015). *Risk and opportunity in an increasingly digital world, insurance governance leadership network, tapestry networks.* Retrieved from https://www.tapestrynetworks.com

Ezeokoli, F. O., Okolie, K. C., Okoye, P. U. & Belonwu, C. C. (2016). Digital transformation in the Nigeria construction industry: The professionals' view. *World Journal of Computer Application and Technology, 4*(1), 23–30.

Ezeokoli, F. O., Ugochukwu, S. C., Agu, N. N., & Akabougu, S. C. (2016). An assessment of the use, benefits and challenges of the 'cash–lite' policy, for construction projects in Anambra State, Nigeria. *European Scientific Journal, 12*(16), 313–328.

Isa, R. B., Jimoh, R. A., & Achuenu, E. (2013). An overview of the contribution of construction sector to sustainable development in Nigeria. *Net Journal of Business Management, 1*(1), 1–6.

Jayaraj, A., & Divakar, H. N. (2018). Robotics in construction industry. *IOP Conference Series: Materials Science and Engineering, 376*(1), 012114. doi:10.1088/1757-8 99X/376/1/012114

MCKinsey. (2016). *Imagining construction's digital future.* Retrieved from https://www.mckinsey.com/capabilities/operations/our-insights/imagining-constructions-digital-future

National Bureau of Statistics (NBS). (2022). *Nigerian gross domestic product report (Q4 2022).* Retrieved from https://nigerianstat.gov.ng/elibrary/read/1241288

Oke, A. E., Aigbavboa, C. O., Stephen, S. S., & Thwala, W. D. (2021). *Sustainable construction in the era of the fourth industrial revolution.* London and New York, NY: Taylor and Francis Group. doi:10.1201/9781003179849-1

Shah, B., Hartman, G., & Whimmple, B. (2014). *CMOs: Time for digital transformation or risk being left on the sidelines.* Retrieved from https://www.accenture.com

Tatum, C. (1989). Organising to increase innovation in construction firms. *Journal of Construction Engineering and Management, 115*(4), 602–617.

World Economic Forum. (2017). Shaping the future of construction: A breakthrough in mindset and technology. Retrieved from https://www.weforum.org/reports/shaping-the-future-of-construction-a-breakthrough-in-mindset-and-technology

Chapter 3

Digital Technologies for Sustainable Infrastructure Management

Abstract

Considering the gradual move into the information age, digital technologies have become the new trend in different industries ranging from agriculture, manufacturing, transportation and banking, among others. The construction industry has also evolved progressively since the last decade to explore and adopt digital transformation considering the immense contribution it has towards productivity. More so, the need to combat global warming has compelled experts to begin to seek new technologies in achieving the green effect. This has led experts and researchers in the industry to seek how digital technologies can help to achieve sustainability and further functional construction. There has been a huge gap as to maximising the impact of digital transformation as many organisations in the industry are still struggling to successfully adopt and implement digital construction. This chapter will help to fill this gap and provide clear insight into how digital can help further sustainable construction.

Keywords: Construction innovation; digital construction; digital technology; digital transformation; sustainable construction; green effect

Introduction

Electronic devices, systems, tools and resources that help to generate store or process data are generally referred to as digital technologies. With complaints growing about the decline in productivity in the construction output, there is a growing paradigm shift towards digitisation to enhance project delivery. Zhan, Pan, Javed, and Chau (2018) believe that digital technologies help in the improvement of construction practices. The growing demand for construction as well as the rising largeness and complexity of structures require that changes must come to the traditional methods and practices in construction (Rajat, Shankar, & Mukund, 2016).

A Digital Path to Sustainable Infrastructure Management, 27–35
Copyright © 2024 Ayodeji E. Oke and Seyi S. Stephen
Published under exclusive licence by Emerald Publishing Limited
doi:10.1108/978-1-83797-703-120241003

Many believe that the implementation of digital technology would bring sustainability to the construction industry. Productivity and cost are the major bases for the change, as continuing with the traditional methods mostly results in a shortage in time not less than 20% of the contractual period. This change in project planning and execution through digital technologies will give room for improved construction in both small and large enterprises (Gough, 2018). Research shows that the construction industry is moving towards maximising the benefits of data-sharing and sustainable technologies, as well as the use of mobile devices. However, there is still a long way to go before the industry can be truly and fully digital. Once this transformation hits its peak, the construction industry and the built industry in general will reap the benefits attached to the adoption of digital technologies into the construction process.

Digitisation in Construction

Plotnikov (2019) defined digitisation as the use of digital technologies in the generating, processing, storing, visualising and transmitting of information towards the development of information. As a result of increased civilisation and changing clients' demand, there has been increasing complexities in construction project and their delivery process. The use of older, inappropriate technologies in the planning and execution of construction projects has caused a lot of problems for construction projects.

This, in the opinion of Ilozor and Kelly (2012) has led to the construction industry being identified as lacking in efficiency, wasteful and very much unproductive. Hence, there is an urgent and progressive need to review and adopt contemporary technologies that are functional towards achieving the project aim. Participants in the construction industry have emphasised the potential that digital technologies promote in the walk towards improving productivity. While other industries such as agriculture, transportation and trading service among others have continued to harness the potential of digital technologies to proffer the best solutions to prevailing problems, the construction industry is largely lagging. However, it is becoming clear to a high percentage of construction professionals that digitisation is the only way to improve productivity.

In Hong Kong, for example, Zhan et al. (2018) reported that the construction industry has been underperforming in terms of productivity; this therefore facilitates the growing trend in the actualisation of digitalisation for the improvement of construction practices. Achieving complete digitalisation in the industry has been hindered due to the disintegrated nature of the construction supply chain. This disintegration continues to act as a speed breaker in the process of digital technology adoption. Even as Madanayake, Senanayake, and Wijayanayake (2019) concluded that gain in productivity is tied to digital transformation when specific skills and knowledge needed to fully take advantage of digital technologies by an organisation are adequately put in place.

Digital Technology

The continuous emergence of digital technology across several sectors has improved operations and outputs simultaneously. Even though there are some concerns about what it causes in terms of demerits, it has been asserted several times that its benefits outweigh the challenges. Some examples of digital technology include online games, mobile phones, multimedia, drones and software, to mention a few. Digital technology makes it possible for large amounts of information to be accumulated on small storage devices that can be easily preserved and transferred. It also improves the speed required in the transmission of data. The positive influence of digitisation can be strongly felt in how people communicate, work and learn. Digital technologies are bringing radical transformations to every industry, without the exception of the construction industry as illustrated by Schweigkofler, Monizza, Domi, Popescu, and Ratajczak (2019).

Digital Technology in Construction

The implementation and adoption of digital technologies in construction have shifted the construction industry from cultural practices directed towards delivery now to that which provide the tendency of sustainability. Also, not only is the shift beneficial to both the clients and the professionals involved, it is a channel through which an increase is experienced in the gross domestic product (GDP) of the country where it is embraced. The built environment in general has witnessed a massive surge in sustainable project delivery over the years, and this has improved the standard of living as well as the whole life cycle of the projects.

In executing construction activities from onset to completion, digital technology plays crucial roles in communication, design, planning, execution and management. This is achieved through the implementation of different social media channels, sustainable technologies in the Fourth Industrial Revolution in the use of robotics, building information modelling (BIM), artificial intelligence (AI), virtual reality, augmented reality, biomimicry, drones, etc. to execute projects within set out budget and duration (Oke, Aigbavboa, Stephen, & Thwala, 2021). Digital technologies were introduced into construction as a means of embracing efficiency within the shortest possible duration. Construction professionals across several fields in the building industry have embraced the technological aspect of involvement in construction as the demands of the clients are ever-increasing. Also, migration from rural areas to urban areas has put pressure on the construction stakeholders to seek alternative practices to provide for the always-growing population within the context of affordability and quality. Several firms and professionals have inculcated the use of digital technologies into their construction and the benefits have been documented to outweigh its challenges (Mohammed, 2020).

Building, in partnership with Ecobuild (2014) in a building digital survey discovered that 70% of construction workers and professionals polled from different roles in the construction industry believed that mobile devices had to a large extent changed the way their company does business. An example of this is

'Interserve's Construction Delivery Application', which allows one to record issues identified on-site on a phone or tablet. Many professionals who have used this application in practice believe it helps to save days of work. Also, another digital technology that has greatly impacted the construction industry is BIM. BIM allows all disciplines to collaborate and be efficient at the same time. Still from the research of Ecobuild (2014), it was discovered that 77% of Architects and 61% of Engineers believe that technology had significantly influenced the way business is carried out in their organisation. Though, a critical examination of this survey shows that there is more adoption of this technology among construction designers, with other disciplines not in tandem with the level of impact accrued to BIM. This could largely be because modelling is more of a design-based tool. This has greatly affected the level of effective use of the software in construction. Only 6.5% of respondents from Ecobuild research agreed to the positive applied impact of on-site digital technologies such as drones and robotics. Consequently, other digital technologies do not seem to have much impact on the industry.

Digital Technology for Sustainable Construction

Different efforts have been made by experts to define sustainability in construction. Ultimately, the meaning of sustainable construction will be subjective based on individuals prevailing local circumstances. Carboni, Duncan, Gonzalez, Milsom, and Young (2018) in the book New Aspects of Surveying opined that: 'How built assets are procured and erected, used and operated, maintained and repaired, modernised and rehabilitated and reused or demolished and recycled constitutes the complete life-cycle of sustainable construction activities'.

The prominence of sustainability as a concept to be taken seriously for practical implementation began in the construction industry in 2011. According to Carboni et al. (2018), sustainability is so important as regards the functionality of the construction industry. More so, construction has been identified as one of the major contributors to carbon emissions. In the last decade, sustainability has risen to prominence on the world stage and the construction industry has been identified as the front-runner as regards pollution and the use of diminishing gas returns. Hence, sustainability has become one of the major focus in the construction industry. For example, in 2013, The Government of the United Kingdom's initiative, Construction 2025, had a target of reducing the rate of carbon emission in the built environment by 50% by the year 2025. Carboni et al. (2018) further reiterated that this scenario is what has led to academic programmes at undergraduate and postgraduate levels now having modules on sustainable development included in their curriculum, and many professionals in the construction industry are seeking to establish their green credentials.

As earlier mentioned regarding the research by Ecobuild (2014), when respondents (clients/occupiers) were asked about which technology their companies are investing in, more than half of clients/occupiers agreed that they were putting money into sustainable technologies. This shows that sustainability is one of the major priorities for the clients. Unlike some professionals, only a few engineers and 31% of consultants agreed that their investments were directed in the wake of sustainable technologies.

Drivers of Digital Technology Application in Construction

Despite the enormous challenges posed by the implementation of digital transformation in the built environment as it has been one of the least digitised industries, several factors from research are inter-playing to drive the application of digital technology in construction. Pan, Linner, Pan, Cheng, and Bock (2020) stated that there is a need for a strategic implementation of digital technologies to help the drivers of digital technology while discouraging the challenges to the implementation of these technologies especially in the construction industry.

In a study by Olanipekun and Sutrisna (2021), some basic drivers of digital technology applications in construction were identified. These drivers were referred to as 'enablers'. Enablers in the researchers' opinion facilitated the successful implementation of digital technologies in construction. These drivers are expressed below:

- Digital culture,
- Digital awareness,
- Legitimation,
- System support,
- Perception and size of the organisation,
- Training opportunities,
- Cost of installation, acquisition and maintenance, etc.

Further study by Stephen (2021) highlighted five major trends acting as drivers of digital technologies application which include:

(1) Embracing automation,
(2) Increased pressure to finish faster and cheaper,
(3) Channelling mobile for real-time communication,
(4) Improved collaboration, and
(5) Concentration on proactive safety.

Challenges of Digital Technology

Despite the current immense positive contribution digital technology has brought to the construction industry, and the great prospect it has to further transform the level of productivity and sustainability in the construction life cycle, there have been challenges in adequately adopting and implementing digital technology.

Some of the barriers to the application of digital technologies include technical, financial and organisational factors as described across several publications.

Despite making progress in its development, the implementation of digital technology has met with concerns on:

- Issues of costing and management (Merschbrock & Munkvold, 2015),
- Security and confidentiality (Kim, Park, & Kim, 2013),
- The problem of resource requirements, and coordination (Wu, Guo, Li, & Zeng, 2016),
- Scepticism because of fragmented nature of the industry (Hartmann et al., 2019),
- Insufficient data and knowledge as another bottleneck to the implementation of digital technology (Palaneeswaran & Kumaraswamy, 2003), and
- Incompatibility or interoperability issues between applications/technologies (Patacas, Dawood, Vukovic, & Kassem, 2015).

Furthermore, in their remarks, Petrov and Hakimov (2019) opined that in order to fully realise the benefits that comes with adopting and implementing digital technologies in construction, executives, skilled employees and other concerned professionals need to embrace the need for change in order to achieve set goals in respect to developing and moving the construction industry forward. However, Oke et al. (2021) highlighted some of the reasons why most acquired digital technologies are either unused at all or underutilised, they include:

- Lack of interface between new and existing systems,
- End users not properly trained,
- Inadequate budget to cover the high number of personnel needed to manage some of these technologies,
- In-system resistance to change, and
- Lack of technical know-how and shortage of support from software developers.

Benefits of Digital Technology for Construction Projects

It is very obvious that digital technologies are full of opportunities in terms of cost efficiency, improve client experience and much more. Many construction experts and professionals are beginning to see the benefits of the adoption and implementation of these technologies in construction practices and processes. In conjunction with the benefits stated by Plotnikov (2019), some of these benefits are expressed below when digital technologies are involved in operations;

- There is competitive advantage which ends in potential growth of profit as a result of dynamisms and flexibility in production process.
- There is the integration of information all through the life cycle of production process which leads to optimisation of production, safety of the environment and new opportunities for business.

- There is a clear and concise interpretation, planning and exactions of activities related to the project.
- Problems that might occur later during the construction are easily identified as early as possible even before the commencement of the project through review platforms enabled by digital technologies.
- In terms of project delivery, standard and value are maximised within the shortest duration and budget with little or no hassle whatsoever.

Parn and Edwards (2019) further stated that digitisation is bringing manufacture, analysis of data, sensing and economy to an advanced level that is bringing about shift in the direction of a smarter, faster and better performing built environment. The researcher concluded that for these benefits to be fully harnessed, this new level of digital transformation must be connected to a dynamic workforce whose knowledge and values will provide a sustainable foundation for digital change.

Conclusion

There is a huge promise of digital technologies bringing about changes that are not envisaged. It has the potential to greatly improve the level of productivity and leaning of the construction process, thus yielding greater profitability. Moreover, it produces great value as regards sustainability, making the built environment and the world at large safer for its inhabitants. There is a speed up in digital technologies, and many construction stakeholders are still resistant to change, and new digital technologies that are taking construction practices one step further in the competitive environment, but we are at that period where every hand must be on deck to digitalise the construction process and practices and develop the digital strategies to ensure successful sustainable construction.

References

Carboni, J., Duncan, W., Gonzalez, M., Milsom, P., & Young, M. (2018). *Sustainable project management: The GPM reference guide*. Retrieved from https://www.ucipfg.com

Ecobuild. (2014). *Ecobuild: Building Research Establishment Environmental Assessment Standard (BREEAM) revamped, new profit scheme*. Retrieved from https://www.constructionmanagement.co.uk

Gough, M. (2018). *Reimagining construction: The vision for digital transformation, and a roadmap for how to get there*. Retrieved from https://www.globalconstruction2030.com

Hartmann, S., Mainka, A., & Stock, W. G. (2019). Opportunities and challenges for civic engagement: A global investigation of innovation competitions. *Civic Engagement and Politics, 3*(4), 607–623.

Ilozor, B. D., & Kelly, D. J. (2012). Building information modelling and integrated project delivery in the commercial construction industry; a conceptual study. *Journal of Engineering, Project, and Production Management, 2*(1), 23–36.

Kim, C., Park, T., & Kim, H. (2013). On-site construction management using mobile computing technology. *Automation in Construction, 35*(4), 415–423. doi:10.1016/j. autcon.2013.05.027

Madanayake, N., Senanayake, S., & Wijayanayake, J. (2019). Digital transformation maturity: A systematic review of literature. *Acta Universitatis Agriculturae et Silviculturae Mendelianae Brunensis, 67*(6), 1565–1578. doi:10.11118/actaun2019670 61565

Merschbrock, C., & Munkvold, B. (2015). Effective digital collaboration in the construction industry–A case study of BIM development in a hospital construction project. *Computers in Industry, 73*(1), 1–7.

Mohammed, S. (2020). *Implementation of digital technology in construction company.* Retrieved from https://www.researchgate.net/publication/344264993

Oke, A. E., Aigbavboa, C. O., Stephen, S. S., & Thwala, W. D. (2021). *Sustainable construction in the era of the fourth industrial revolution.* London and New York, NY: Taylor and Francis Group. doi:10.1201/9781003179849-1

Olanipekun, A. O., & Sutrisna, M. (2021). Facilitating digital transformation in construction—a systematic review of the current state of the art. *Frontiers in Built Environment, 7*(2), 660758. doi:10.3389/fbuil.2021.660758

Palaneeswaran, E., & Kumaraswamy, M. (2003). Knowledge mining of information sources for research in construction management. *Journal of Construction Engineering and Management, 129*(2), 182–191.

Pan, M., Linner, T., Pan, W., Cheng, H., & Bock, T. (2020). Structuring the context for construction robot development through integrated scenario approach. *Automation in Construction, 114*(7), 103174. doi:10.1016/j.autcon.2020.103174

Parn, E. A., & Edwards, D. (2019). Cyber threats confronting the digital built environment: Common data environment vulnerabilities and block chain deterrence. *Engineering Construction and Architectural Management, 26*(2), 245–256.

Patacas, J., Dawood, N., Vukovic, V., & Kassem, M. (2015). BIM for facilities management: Evaluating BIM standards in asset register creation and service life planning. *Journal of Information Technology in Construction, 20*(2), 313–331.

Petrov, I., & Hakimov, A. (2019). Digital technologies in construction monitoring and construction control. *IOP Conference Series: Materials Science and Engineering, 497*(1), 012016. Retrieved from https://www.iopscience.iop.org

Plotnikov, V. A. (2019). Digitalization and modernization of the national employment policy. *Economics and Management, 1*(11), 87–94. doi:10.35854/1998-1627-2019-10-87-94

Rajat, A., Shankar, C., & Mukund, S. (2016). *Imagining construction's digital future.* Retrieved from https://www.mckinsey.com

Schweigkofler, A., Monizza, G. P., Domi, E., Popescu, A., & Ratajczak, J. (2019). Development of a digital platform based on the integration of augmented reality and BIM for the management of information in construction processes. In *15th IFIP International Conference on product Lifecycle Management (PLM).* July 2018. Turin, Italy (pp. 46–55). doi:10.1007/978-3-030-01614-2_5

Stephen, D. (2021). *5 construction industry trends driving digital transformation.* Retrieved from https://www.smartsheet.com/content-center/executive-center/digital-transformation/5-construction-industry-trends-driving-digital-transformation-infographic

Wu, J., Guo, S., Li, J., & Zeng, D. (2016). Bio data meet green challenges: Big data toward green applications. *Institute of Electrical and Electronics Engineers (IEEE) Systems Journal, 10*(3), 888–900.

Zhan, W., Pan, W., Javed, A. A., & Chau, K. W. (2018). Correlation analysis of key influencing factors to the total factor productivity of the Hong Kong construction industry. In *Proceedings of the 21st International Symposium on Advancement of Construction Management and Real Estate*, January 6–8, China. doi:10.1007/978-981-10-6190-5_51

Chapter 4

Connected Machines for Sustainable Infrastructure Management

Abstract

Connected machines are the automation of several types of machines connected towards beneficial growth of sustainable construction especially in the era of the Fourth Industrial Revolution. This chapter gave an insight into the emergence of digitalisation in the construction sector and the importance of connected machines in sustainable construction. It further elucidated its mode of operations, devices applicable, drivers and challenges for its full application in construction and benefits on construction projects. It finally gave a conclusion on its urgent need for full incorporation due to its technological benefits for present and future construction works.

Keywords: Connected construction; connected machines; devices; digitalisation; Internet of Things; sustainable construction

Introduction

The significant change in this present day is at a fast speed when compared to the past since activities are now mostly automated through different channels. The developments in technology and innovation are making work easier with the combination of different technological practices which is often termed the Internet of Things (IoT). The period from the 1970s to 1980s centralised on connecting computers while the 1990s–2000s was characterised by connecting people; it is worthy of note that the period of 2010s to this time focuses on connecting everything to the internet.

The development of human knowledge in this present era is channelled towards construction by building powerful devices and machines which may either be physically big or small. An increase in knowledge daily is working towards minimising effort expended on daily activities physically through the provision of machines that are connected that control these activities remotely

A Digital Path to Sustainable Infrastructure Management, 37–46
Copyright © 2024 Ayodeji E. Oke and Seyi S. Stephen
Published under exclusive licence by Emerald Publishing Limited
doi:10.1108/978-1-83797-703-120241004

within the shortest possible time. The functionality of these machines extended to the construction sector has led to digitalising the sector. It has been observed that the sector is responding to changes in digitalisation when compared to previous years; as it is also of the expectation that more records will be made in years to come in terms of adoption and actualisation, especially in the built industry (Agarwal, Chandrasekaran, & Sridhar, 2016).

Digitalisation in the construction sector is accrued to the assemblage of machines connected to perform certain functions; some of the machines executing various activities on site today are groups of different machines connected to make a single entity. Some of these construction machines can be remotely operated using wireless protocols like wireless fidelity (Wi-Fi) technology connected to the various machines which makes them work faster and increase productivity with lesser construction project duration.

Digitalisation in Construction

Digitalisation can be referred to as a method of digital technologies for improving the productivity and value of a product within a company for customer attraction, satisfaction and effective delivery. Digitalisation is a powerful tool that changes the structures, processes and systems of a company (Plekhanov & Netland, 2019).

Digitalisation accrued many benefits to the construction industry when fully utilised. These benefits come in enhancing better information, profit maximisation and sustainability improvement (Hilty & Aebischer, 2015). Considering these potentials and others to be gained, it is obvious that construction digitalisation is an indispensable key to sustainability in the construction sector. A wide range of these innovations has surfaced over time with several opinions maintaining that they will benefit the construction industry and as well minimise pitfalls in construction project delivery and productivity. Some parts of these innovations are; unmanned aerial vehicles (UAVs), building information modelling (BIM), artificial intelligence (AI), augmented reality (AR), IoT, 3D printing, etc. (Ghosh, Edwards, & Hosseini, 2020; Oke, AigbavboaStephen, & Thwala, 2021; Romdhane & El-Sayegh, 2020; York, Al-Bayati, & Al-Shabbani, 2020).

The construction sector is one of the drivers of the nation's economy. Even with this, the industry has been bedevilled with problems relating to performance in terms of low productivity, hyper construction cost, inadequate site safety records, unsatisfactory project performance, inadequate creativity and innovation, low sustainability practice and so on (Fathalizadeh et al., 2021; Ghodoosi, Bagchi, Hosseini, Vilutien, & Zeynalian, 2021; Hosseini, Banihashemi, Martek, Golizadeh, & Ghodoosi, 2018; Leviäkangas, MokPaik, & Moon, 2017). In a bid to solve these problems, various efforts have been put in motion to eliminate occurrences that might deter the implementation and adoption of digitalisation into the built industry as a whole (Gruszka, Jupp, & DeValence, 2020; Loosemore, 2020). Benefits to be derived from digitalisation over time in the construction sector will include but are not limited to customer expectancies development, springing up of a new generation of professionals, technology advancement opportunities, the rapid growth of new companies within the sector, unfolding of new infrastructures and provision of new legal structure (Stoyanova, 2020).

Connected Machines

Machines comprise of elements or components assembled or created to perform specific functions. Each component or element assembled operates simple actions towards functionality while the whole machine system operates complex and useful functions. The modes of operations of some of these machines are depicted in Fig. 1.

Various connected machines in today's worlds are numerous due to the day-to-day technology advancement and quest for IoT. The IoT comprises of inter-connected computing machines and objects which are linked together with devices such as Bluetooth, satellite, radio frequency identification (RFID), Wi-Fi, near field communication (NFC), ZigBee, Z-wave, etc.

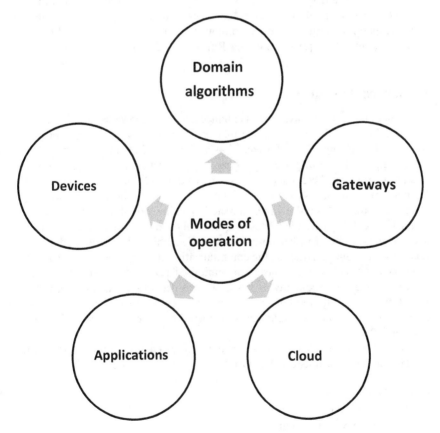

Fig. 1.   Mode of Operations of Connected Machines.

The IoT-connected machines are applicable for monitoring and analysis of real-time data such as factor digitalisation, logistic and inventory management, product flow monitoring and others. Some of the applicable devices for IoT-connected machines are:

- Sensors,
- Actuators, and
- Appliances coupled with gadgets that can be installed into mobile devices, environmental sensors, industrial equipment, medical devices and others.

There are various types of connected machines in today's world based on application and functions, some of these types are:

- Flywheel friction welding and continuous friction welding which is applicable to mechanical activities in a machine (Sathiya & Noorul Haq, 2008; Welding Handbook, 1980),
- Torque converter, variable-speed wind turbine (Carlin et al., 2003), and
- Some other available connected machines but not limited to these include smart phones, game consoles, computer, tablets, smart wristwatch, smart Google, etc. (Banerjee, Alleman, & Rappoport, 2013).

Connected Machines in Construction

Construction processes have gained enhancement over the years due to the advent of technology which has yielded an increase in productivity and ease of project delivery. This change is not farfetched as various connected machines or devices have been developed and are still in use in construction processes for projected execution. Some of these machines or devices aid in the collection of data, analyse them and send messages to other machines to be aware of the activities within and outside a domain. Also, this can be directed to an individual to function regarding safety by providing possible routes to a location or monitoring possible danger on a construction site. Furthermore, connected machines have reduced the time taken to carry out activities as the communication time between the construction phase and project delivery has been minimised (Ostroukh, 2013; Ostroukh & Surkova, 2015). Subsequently, it has been recorded to have a function in transportation for mining and construction works such as the transmission of heavy buses, tractors, vehicles, tanks, railway locomotives, etc. (Antsev, Trushin, & Plyasov, 2020).

Some of the available connected machines that have brought digitalisation into road construction as illustrated by Ostroukh, Kotliarskiy, and Sarychev, 2019 are:

- Articulated hauler,
- Wheel loader payload system,
- Excavator payload system,
- 3D grading system, etc.

Others are smart boot, smart clothes, smart gloves, drone, close circuit cameras, etc. applicable in monitoring and tracking potential hazards and emergencies on construction sites.

Connected Machines for Sustainable Construction

Construction projects are most times complex that involves the consumption of a huge amount of resources. The resultant products of the industry also consume much energy which is often detrimental to the occupants in the long run. This, therefore, brought about the need for sustainability in construction works. Meanwhile, the rapid response of innovation and technology in today's world has eased the challenges of sustaining construction projects through technology devices that are interconnected to moderate the use of resources by adopting comprehensive design, construction, operation and maintenance for its operations.

Various machines have emerged as a result of severally connected machines to regulate, maintain and control construction in the wake of sustainability. As summarised in Table 1, some of these machines have sensors or are controlled in automation that aids in the adjustment of room temperature, heating, ventilation and air condition (HVAC), and measure electric power; the programmable logic controllers (PLC) that controls indoor environment automatically, save building energy and improve occupant's convenience; programmable sensitive control door, building information modelling, prefabricated and modular construction, a smart lighting system that manages light sensors by regulating lighting and control luminosity; and smart elevator which changes routes subject to occupant's direction among others.

Drivers of Connected Machines Application in Construction

The application of connected machines is yet to gain much popularity in construction despite its accrued advantages to the present and future generations. Meanwhile, the Fourth Industrial Revolution has exposed the construction sector to the idea of connected machines through which machines and devices are connected for ease of activities execution and conveniences which are gradually leading to a smart world.

The studies by Bharadwaj, ElSawy, Pavlou, and Venkatraman (2013) and Matt, Hess, and Benlian (2015) identified some various drivers to the full adoption of connected machines in the construction industry. These are:

- Privacy,
- Security,
- Scale,
- Scope,
- Value creation and speed of incorporation,
- Supply chain orchestration,
- Decision-making,

Table 1. Showing Parts/Elements of Connected Machines and Their Functions.

Machine Parts/Systems	Functions
Sensor	• Room temperature, heating, ventilation and air condition (HVAC) regulation • Electric power measurement
Programmable Logic Controllers (PLC)	• Automatic indoor environment control • Building energy conservation • occupant's convenience improvement
Programmable Sensitive Control Door (PSCD)	• Security provision • Durability
Building Information Modelling (BIM)	• Building efficiency • Evaluation and estimation • Swift project delivery • Reduces stress • Error detection, etc.
Prefabricated and Modular Construction (PMC)	• Enhance project delivery • Fast completion period • Material wastage management • Cost reduction, etc.
Smart Lighting System (SLS)	• Manages light sensors by regulating lighting • Control luminosity
Smart elevator	Changes routes subject to occupant's direction

- Product launching,
- Adoption of model for its development in terms of structural changes,
- Utilisation of technology,
- Changes in value creation and financial perspectives,
- Awareness,
- Ease of operation,
- Electricity,
- Employment opportunities to operators in terms of installation, etc.

Challenges of Connected Machines

Every development, innovation and idea has faced some challenges during its implementation stage. The incorporation of smart connected machines involves interconnected devices and data collection, difficulty is somewhat faced in installation and operation due to many factors/challenges. Some of the challenges that may arise in the incorporation of these machines as stated by Izabela, Anna, and Roman (2016), Molavi and Barral (2016), Dawood and Iqbal (2010), Ling (2003), Tagaza and Wilson (2004) are:

- Level of literacy,
- Adaptation to changes by users,
- Lack of skilful personnel,
- Network accessibility,
- Cost of purchase and installation,
- Availability of devices and material for the design,
- Slow rate of incorporation by construction sector,
- Procurement management system which involves the collaboration of the contractor and the supplier;
- Cost of licencing the software involved,
- Cultural resistance to adaptation,
- Technical compatibility in transporting data storage,
- Technical difficulties at construction stage,
- Risk involved due to different forms of contracts available for the project, and
- Interest and communication differences among project members, etc.

Benefits of Connected Machines for Construction Projects

Researches and findings have revealed that application of connected machines to construction projects have numerous benefits attached to it. In white paper report delivered by Srivastav (2021) on benefits of connected machines to construction and engineering industries, the details of these benefits are described briefly below:

- *Predictive Equipment Maintenance*: connected machines helps in notifying and communicating requirements for equipment maintenance thereby cutting down unforeseen breakdown before expiration of lifespan and increase the scrap value of equipment at disposal.
- *Increase Site Productivity*: the possibility of this occur as it aids in tracking, monitoring and preventing theft on construction site which usually happens on large construction project. It functions when sensors are installed on various equipment on site as it gives information of travelled distance of site assets.
- *Improved Utilisation of Equipment*: best use of equipment is important for project cost minimisation so as to compete favourably in the construction sector as this will help in reducing the number of equipment deployed to site during construction execution. This is visible through transmitting of data like engine-on hours by installed devices which assist the project manager to know the real-time equipment utilisation on construction project sites. This is important in equipment allocation and thus gives room for desired decisions to be adopted towards safe equipment breakdown and cost.
- *Reduction in Fuel Consumption*: sensors mounted on equipment will help to minimise fuel wastage and theft on project sites. Machines and equipment

devouring fuel that mounted with sensors will give information on any fuel consumption spikes that occurs through the data received through the devices of connected machines. An alert will automatically be sent to the concerned site engineer to take further actions in case of such occurrence.

Furthermore, connected machines aid in safety enhancement and provide adequate information for documentations for future purposes. It also aid in energy consumption within the surroundings of a building or construction project which gives cost reduction, effective productivity and healthy lifestyle to individuals on site, home within the immediate environment.

Conclusion

The benefits and the usefulness of connected machines in this digital world are indispensable especially as most sectors of the economy are mostly centred towards digitalisation. The construction industry needs to take prompt action in leveraging this concept as the products have proven more beneficial in productivity, time, cost optimisation and sustainability. Challenges faced in the construction industry must be tackled within the possible time as the industry cannot achieve its best in this revolutionary period without getting connected. It is also important for individuals to avail the opportunities of interconnected machines to give a better living for this generation and the ones to come in terms of project construction because of its health benefits and future maintenance cost of any construction put in place. Also, governments in both developed and developing countries need to develop a framework that will pave the way for ease digitalising of the construction industry within their domain.

References

Agarwal, R., Chandrasekaran, S., & Sridhar, M. (2016). *Imagining construction's digital future.* Retrieved from https://www.mckinsey.com

Antsev, V. Y., Trushin, N. N., & Plyasov, A. V. (2020). Improving energy performance of hydraulic torque converters. *Journal of Physics, 15*(46), 012–124. doi:10.1088/1742- 6596/1546/1/012124

Banerjee, A., Alleman, J., & Rappoport, P. (2013). Video-viewing behavior in the era of connected devices. *Communications and Strategies, 1*(1), 19–42.

Bharadwaj, A., ElSawy, O. A., Pavlou, P. A., & Venkatraman, N. (2013). Digital business strategy: Toward a next generation of insights. *Maintenance Information System for Quality, 37*(4), 471–482.

Carlin, A. S., Laxson, E. B., & Muljadi, K. (2003). The history and state of the art of variable- speed wind turbine. *Wind Energy, 6*(4), 129–159. doi:10.1002/we.77

Dawood, N., & Iqbal, N. (2010). Building information modelling (BIM): A visual and whole life cycle approach, CONVR2010. In K. Makanae, N. Yabuki, & K. Kashiyama (Eds.), *Proceedings of the 10th International Conference on Construction Applications of Virtual Reality, CONVR2010 Organizing Committee,* Sendai, Japan, November 4–5 (pp. 7–14).

Fathalizadeh, A., Hosseini, M. R., Vaezzadeh, S. S., Edwards, D. J., Martek, I., & Shooshtarian, S. (2021). Barriers to sustainable construction project management: The case of Iran. *Smart and Sustainable Built Environment, 2*(1), 1–24. doi:10.1108/SASBE-09-2020-0132

Ghodoosi, F., Bagchi, A., Hosseini, M. R., Vilutien, E. T., & Zeynalian, M. (2021). Enhancement of bid decision-making in construction projects: A reliability analysis approach. *Journal of Civil Engineering and Management, 27*(2), 149–161.

Ghosh, A., Edwards, D. J., & Hosseini, M. R. (2020). Patterns and trends in internet of Things (IoT) research: Future applications in the construction industry. *Engineering Construction and Architectural Management, 28*(2), 457–481.

Gruszka, A., Jupp, J. R., & DeValence, G. (2020). Digital foundations: How technology is transforming Australia's construction sector. Retrieved from https://opus.lib.uts.edu.au/handle/10453/124861

Hilty, L. M., & Aebischer, B. (2015). ICT for sustainability: An emerging research field. In *ICT innovations for sustainability* (pp. 3–36). Berlin/Heidelberg, Germany: Springer.

Hosseini, M. R., Banihashemi, S., Martek, I., Golizadeh, H., & Ghodoosi, F. (2018). Sustainable delivery of mega projects in Iran: Integrated model of contextual factors. *Journal of Management in Engineering, 34*(2), 05017011. doi:10.1061/(ASCE)ME.1943-5479.0000587

Izabela, H., Anna, G., & Roman, P. (2016). 3D printing of buildings and building components as the future of sustainable construction? *Procedia Engineering, 15*(3), 292–299. doi:10.1016/j.proeng.2016.07.357

Leviäkangas, P., MokPaik, S., & Moon, S. (2017). Keeping up with the pace of digitization: The case of the Australian construction industry. *Technological Society, 50*(1), 33–43.

Ling, J. U. (2003). *The project manager's personal characteristic, skills and roles in local construction industry.* Published Master's dissertation, Faculty of Civil Engineering, University Technology Malaysia, Malaysia.

Loosemore, M. (2020). *Australia's construction industry must unite around a cohesive strategy.* Retrieved from https://www.thefifthestate.com.au/innovation/building-construction/australias-construction-industry-must-unite-around-acohesive-strategy/

Matt, C., Hess, T., & Benlian, A. (2015). Digital transformation strategies. *Business and Information Systems Engineering, 57*(6), 339–343.

Molavi, J., & Barral, D. L. (2016). A construction procurement method to achieve sustainability in modular construction. *Procedia Engineering, 145*(7), 1362–1369.

Oke, A. E., Aigbavboa, C. O., Stephen, S. S., & Thwala, W. D. (2021). *Sustainable construction in the era of the fourth industrial revolution.* London and New York, NY: Taylor and Francis Group. doi:10.1201/9781003179849-1

Ostroukh, A. V. (2013). *Systems of artificial intelligence in the industry, the robotics and the transport complex.* Limited, Krasnoyarsk, Siberia: Publishing House Science and Innovation Center.

Ostroukh, A., Vasiliev, Y., Kotliarskiy, E., & Sarychev, I. (2019). Connected quarry machines digital systems. *ARPN Journal of Engineering and Applied Sciences, 14*(1), 135–140.

Ostroukh, A. V., & Surkova, N. E. (2015). *Intelligence information systems and technologies.* Limited, Krasnoyarsk, Siberia: Publishing House Science and Innovation Center.

Plekhanov, D., & Netland, T. (2019). Digitalization stages in firms: Towards a framework. In *Proceedings of the 26th EurOMA Conference,* June 17–19, Helsinki, Finland.

Romdhane, L., & El-Sayegh, S. M. (2020). 3D printing in construction: Benefits and challenges. *International Journal of Structural and Civil Engineering Resources,* 9(3), 314–317.

Sathiya, P., & Noorul Haq, A. (2008). Some experimental investigations on friction welded stainless steel joints. *Materials and Design,* 29(6), 1099–1109.

Srivastav, N. (2021). *Whitepaper: Connected machines in the engineering and construction industry.* Retrieved from https://www.google.com/connected-machines

Stoyanova, M. (2020). Good practices and recommendations for success in construction digitalization. *Technology, Education, Management Journal,* 9(1), 42–47. doi:10.18421/TEM91-07

Tagaza, E., & Wilson, J. L. (2004). *Green buildings: Drivers and barriers E lessons learned from five Melbourne developments.* Report Prepared for Building Commission by University of Melbourne and Business Outlook and Evaluation, Australia.

Welding Handbook. (1980). Resistance and solid state welding and other joining processes, AWS, Miami. *Material and Design,* 58(76), 239–262.

York, D. D., Al-Bayati, A. J., & Al-Shabbani, Z. Y. (2020). Potential applications of UAV within the construction industry and the challenges limiting implementation. In *Construction research congress: Project management and controls, materials, and contracts, 2020* (pp. 31–39). Reston, VA: American Society of Civil Engineers.

Chapter 5

Ecological Economics for Sustainable Infrastructure Management

Abstract

Ecological economics is a multidisciplinary endeavour to connect the social sciences and nature in general. It also connects aspects of ecology and economics to a particular understanding. The created concept centred on the mission to acquire a more advanced albeit better scientific understanding of the complex interconnections between humans, animals and the rest of nature. This is driven towards utilising the obtained knowledge to establish policies that will lead to a more environmentally sustainable world, with a fair resource distribution (both across human groups and generations, as well as between humans, the environment and other species), and also efficiently allocates limited resources such as 'natural' and 'social' capital. This practice necessitates the development of new methodologies that are comprehensive, adaptive, integrative, multi-scale, pluralistic and evolutionary, while also acknowledging the enormous uncertainties involved.

Keywords: Construction economics; construction environment; economies; green construction; sustainability; sustainable construction

Introduction

One of the most important economic industries is the construction industry, employing millions of people. However, analogue technologies continue to drive it, which has been critical to its decades-long success. As a result, digitalisation is only gradually making its way into firms' tried-and-true procedures. Many of them would rather cling to 2D technology than use 3D models for visualisation or planning projects using comfortable analogue tools rather than risky digital alternatives. As a result of this rising movement towards the usage of digital technology in the construction sector, construction businesses are seeking remedial solutions to difficulties. Construction professionals can profit from numerous technological advancements in project delivery, according to evidence. They can

A Digital Path to Sustainable Infrastructure Management, 47–55
Copyright © 2024 Ayodeji E. Oke and Seyi S. Stephen
Published under exclusive licence by Emerald Publishing Limited
doi:10.1108/978-1-83797-703-120241005

profit from numerous technological advancements in project delivery. This will eradicate challenges such as cost overruns, errors in designs and planning, substandard projects, project delays and so on. Technological practices are introduced in the form of automated and self-driven devices, applications, etc. in the form of virtual reality (VR), robotics, decision support systems (DSS), Internet of Things (IoT), Internet of Everything (IoE), augmented reality (AR), 3D printing, building information modelling (BIM), unmanned aerial vehicles (UAVs), among others, and are therefore targeting the implementation of sustainable practices into construction and other industries that makes up the economy (Oke, Aigbavboa, Stephen, & Thwala, 2021).

The notion of ecological economics (EE) is a relevant source of resource management difficulties within the sustainability of the construction industry. Ecological economics is concerned with the interactions between ecosystems and economic systems. With rising environmental deterioration, environmental issues are gaining relevance in the construction industry around the world. As a result, as part of enterprise risk management, it is becoming increasingly important for construction firms to proactively manage environmental aspects of projects during the building, operation and demolition stages (Ruževicius, 2010). When it comes to addressing environmental concerns, the construction industry has been proactive. This reveals a lack of appropriate mitigation of negative repercussions, which jeopardises gains associated with infrastructure expansion and development.

Digitalisation in Construction

Construction has improved immensely over the years from the use of traditional materials and equipment to more advanced and technological devices to plan, design, monitor and implement executions of programmes within the scheme of work about a particular project (Oke, Aigbavboa, & Ndou, 2018). This change experienced has been discussed to be a result of the growing population in the world and the need for continuous housing. Not only this, in the quest to find evolvement (an integral part of humans) from current practices, the construction professionals had to develop alternatives in the total construction process to meet the ever-increasing demands of the clients. To achieve this, the Fourth Industrial Revolution (adoption of technology into construction) has been touted to bridge the gap in cost, efficiency and management of construction projects in regards to profits, quality, quantity, whole life cycle, functionalities, etc. (Oke et al., 2021) as summarised in Fig. 1.

Ecological Economies for Sustainable Construction

Most construction firms and property developers in the developing world are driven by short-term cost-benefit calculations, so incorporating environmental issues into buildings is not very popular. Environmental challenges have been discussed for a while now across several disciplines, yet, some still feel the danger

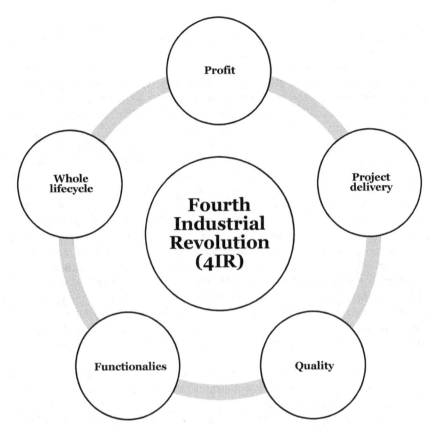

Fig. 1.   Fourth Industrial Revolution (4IR) Aiding Construction.

posed by these challenges is infinitesimal. Some professionals believe that combating or introducing ecological safety practices into construction is a waste of resources and capital that would have been used for other sections of the project.

The built industry has a large ecological footprint and is heavily resource reliant in all of its activities. The materials used in the industry are sourced from nature as well as other fabricated types within the context of specific functions. This is further explained by that the usage of the enormous material by the construction industry is correspondingly causing major havoc to the environment. Furthermore, excessive resource usage is likely to harm the sector, even as it exacerbates environmental degradation. The challenges connected with building at the source are addressed by including environmental concerns in infrastructure development. It aims to reduce the use of non-renewable resources, improve the natural environment and eliminate the use of pollutants (Holmes & Hudson, 2000). It is a fantastic solution that quickly pays for itself. When an additional infrastructure network is yet to be created or expanded in emerging countries, the future of problems related to degradation and irresponsible natural resource usage looks bleak.

With the limited coverage currently available, the ecological footprint is disproportionately large; if this trend continues, the consequences appear unappealing if developing countries continue to develop in an unsustainable manner. External environmental costs and negative externalities are enormous for a sector whose activities are resource-dependent and linked to a wide range of negative environmental impacts, thus environmental management systems (EMS) are essential as a tool for mitigating environmental consequences and instilling sustainability (Cole, 2005). With rising environmental deterioration, environmental issues are gaining relevance in the construction industry around the world. As a result, as part of enterprise risk management, it is becoming increasingly important for construction firms to proactively manage environmental aspects of projects during the building, operation and demolition stages. Unlike manufacturing companies, few construction companies have fully adopted an EMS, according to Oke et al. (2018). This is due to the manufacturing sector's long-term stability and the continued focus on environmental control in this sector. Environmental management policies, laws and multilateral environmental agreements (MEAs) have previously focused on the manufacturing and agricultural industries, but as more people become aware of the negative and long-term effects of the construction industry, environmental MEAs are looping in the construction sector.

Construction enterprises, in contrast to manufacturing companies that are proactive in monitoring their environmental consequences, are late adopters of EMS. Manufacturing industries have reaped numerous benefits associated with EMS, including improved regulatory compliance, improved stakeholder/client relationships and the reduction and opening of trade barriers, easing international trade as 'eco-citizenship' that allows every sector to participate in the green economy (Daneke, Lenox, & Hall, 2010). Reduced costs and risks have also been achieved as a result of sustainable resource consumption and production. Continents that have successfully mainstreamed EMS into their construction sector attribute the decision to policies, government pressure and market competition. Due to their global export concentration, Asia and Europe have made EMS a procurement policy need, and suppliers must be ISO-accredited.

Developing countries must accelerate the implementation of EMS to preserve and expand access to global markets and collaborations. Many developing countries are promoting uptake by partially covering certification expenses. To close the loop in the building industry, the finance sector has greater clout than policy in catalysing and sustaining growth (Oke et al., 2021). The financial sector is critical to the development of a comprehensive green economy and the smooth transition from brown to green growth. Because of green funding, EMS in construction projects in industrialised countries is more complex. Low-interest funds are used to fund green projects that are environmentally sound.

Lending agencies and banks that offer green finance have carbon credit advisory services to guide clients on clean development mechanisms (CDM) and voluntary emission reductions (VER) as part of broader efforts to sustainably nurture and future-proof the economy, as well as mainstream social and environmental considerations in developed countries. They also offer structured instruments that provide upfront funding for carbon credit receivables. Brown projects are not financed in the same way as green initiatives are. This obligates the developer to carry out a project in an environmentally friendly manner (Oke et al., 2018).

The United Kingdom has shown tremendous leadership in this area and has established a Green Investment Bank to help fund it. In addition, the United Kingdom has created The Green Book, which explains 'how to combine economic, financial, social, and environmental assessments of a policy, program, or project'. However, in emerging countries, the finance sector wields considerable authority to enable projects to meet and surpass regulatory standards. This may help to overcome the industry's inertia when it comes to environmental performance. South Korea has encouraged the purchase of energy-saving gadgets by providing low-interest financing (Bina, 2013).

Governments can encourage adoption by cutting or eliminating taxes on environmentally friendly technologies, equipment and accessories. The tariffs on imported wastewater treatment equipment have been cut in Indonesia, a developing country. China, a pioneer in green financing in the developing world, encourages the use of pollution control technology by providing tax breaks and exemptions.

Challenges of Ecological Economies

When it comes to addressing environmental concerns, the construction industry has been proactive. This reveals a lack of appropriate mitigation of negative repercussions described in Fig. 2, which jeopardises gains associated with infrastructure expansion and development. According to Ding (2008), the construction sector's poor performance is attributable to waste of capital (both natural and fiscal) and labour. Furthermore, developing countries over-rely on end-of-pipe technologies, which is still attributed to a reactive approach to problem-solving, a lack of government and client pressure, subcontracting practices that weaken and dilute EMS implementation, low awareness, high implementation costs and a lack of/inadequate top management support in firms. As a result, the purchase of energy-saving and water-saving equipment is low, which is aggravated by a financial and tax environment that does not encourage the adoption of these technologies. In poor countries, there are also competing needs for subsidies. Food insecurity, for example, has led to the subsidisation of food commodities, which has been exacerbated by climate change. The burden placed on emerging economies does not make subsidising foreign waste management systems any easier.

Infrastructure development does not take population increase into account. When the population was lower, sewer pipes and solid waste processing systems were established. Their capability is insufficient to deal with the population

Fig. 2.   Challenges Facing the Implementation of Ecological
Economies (EE) in Construction.

growth and its accompanying repercussions, let alone the demands. In addition, in many developing countries, insufficient training and skill development is a barrier to EMS adoption and implementation in the construction sector. This has an impact on the proper assessment of project activities that are out of character with the environment and the prescription of relevant mitigation measures (Barker, 2013).

Also, green building is considered costly because the necessary technologies, materials and know-how are not widely available in underdeveloped nations. To lower premiums paid to engineers, green building-accredited professionals and architects, the learning curve of professionals familiar with sustainable construction techniques and technology has yet to flatten (Oke et al., 2018). In poor nations, fewer specialists are familiar with green building technology, EMS and local contractors who can build green. Green construction materials and technology are sometimes viewed with scepticism. Incorporating green interventions from the start (during design) reduces costs even more than adding green 'add-ons' after the project is completed. Developers in underdeveloped countries, on the other hand, incorporate green measures during or near the completion phases of projects, making them costly and prohibitive (Windapo, 2014).

The conventional separation of design and construction activities in under-developed nations impedes environmental performance since the contractor has little input in material and technology selection. Because country environmental legislation and policies are not updated to reflect current and future needs, and they are also purposely vague and inexplicit, thus policy support for EMS adoption in the construction sector in developing nations is shaky. The break-down of environmental legislation by industry is insufficient or non-existent. Furthermore, the execution of the programme is hampered by corruption and a lack of cooperation among various government departments with overlapping powers (Hassan et al., 2022). In addition, responsible agencies are underfunded, understaffed and undertrained to effectively carry out their missions (shared and specific). They are spread too thin due to a lack of resources to implement rules and regulations, resulting in organised chaos and a lack of commitment to environmental performance, which is regarded as a non-issue by many.

Building and construction enforcement for environmental and social compliance is low or absent, especially in industries that are primarily government-managed or with politician investments (Cohen, 2006). Because of this lack of environmental and social responsibility, non-government contractors are under less obligation to adopt and execute EMS. Furthermore, even at the top, limited awareness of and interest in ISO 14001 certification has an impact on private sector actors, informing consistent behaviour in the industry. The acceptance of the ISO 9001 series by the government has motivated non-government organisations to get it, and the same can be said for ISO 14001 series.

Governments must raise the bar by setting an example in terms of resource use and waste management. The previous command-and-control strategy will be supported by government projects and premises, which will include incentives to enhance compliance, assist conservation and maintain economic growth and returns.

Benefits of Ecological Economies (EE)

The impacts of the implementation of EMS construction projects by organisations have been seen to be able to:

- Identify hazards at an early stage,
- Reduce costs and overruns,
- Allow projects to be completed on schedule,
- Increase product confidence,
- Provide competitive advantage,
- Monetary savings,
- Sustainable resource consumption,

- Improved health,
- Reduction in gaseous exchange,
- Manage wastes (liquid and solid),
- Enhance efficiency in process and execution, and
- Improve budget.

Ecological economies can help to mitigate the construction industry's environmental impact. The benefits of ecological development are typically intangible; they only become apparent over time, with lower operating costs and a clear environmental and social influence on the surrounding community. In the study by Ruževicius (2010), in terms of addressing or combating environmental deterioration, it was stated that the implementation of several ecological administrations by the state, federal and other concerned policymakers about the essentiality of ecological economics will go a long way in achieving benefits mentioned before, as well as facilitate the adoption of the process into construction planning, design and execution.

Drivers of Ecological Economies

Having highlighted benefits related to the implementation of EMS into construction, drivers that either facilitate swift or slow adoption are expressed below (Oke et al., 2018):

- New ideas should be shared (environmental campaigns, conferences, etc.).
- Encourage people to come up with new ideas for sustainable construction.
- Changing the minimal percentage of sustainability legislation in a design (green construction).
- Advertising (promotes the use of 'green' products and structures through the media).
- Labelling on a voluntary basis (aiding customers to recognise and understand values attached to green buildings through a third party rating system).
- Exemptions from environmental taxes are being reduced.
- Reporting on the company (informing consumers on the social and environmental values of each individual product).
- Putting policy tools together (merging and formulating functional strategies that will cover wastes, energy, production and transportation, etc. into a single broad policy in targeted fiscal years).
- Changing bidding procedure to involve green-enabled practices.
- Resources are limited (perceptible regulations on available resources).

Conclusion

Developing countries most times rely on end-of-pipe technologies, and this is attributed to a reactive approach to problem-solving, a lack of government and client pressure, subcontracting practices that weaken and dilute EMS implementation, low awareness, high implementation costs and a lack of/inadequate top management support in firms. In addition, building and construction enforcement for environmental and social compliance is low or absent, especially in industries that are primarily government-managed or with politician investments. Because of this lack of environmental and social responsibility, non-government contractors are under less obligation to adopt and execute EMS. It is therefore recommended that government must raise the bar by setting an example in terms of resource usage and waste management. This can be achieved when the government gives incentives to project executed within EMS, and this will enhance compliance, assist conservation and maintain economic growth and returns.

References

Barker, T. (2013). *What is ecological economics, as distinct from the neoclassical environmental economics?* University of Cambridge.

Bina, O. (2013). The green economy and sustainable development: An uneasy balance? *Environment and Planning C: Government and Policy, 31*(6), 1023–1047.

Cohen, M. J. (2006). Sustainable consumption research as democratic expertise. *Journal of Consumer Policy, 29*(1), 67–77.

Cole, R. J. (2005). Building environmental assessment methods: Redefining intentions and roles. *Building Research & Information, 35*(5), 455–467.

Daneke, G. A., Lenox, M. J., & Hall, J. K. (2010). Sustainable development and entrepreneurship: Past contributions and future directions. *Journal of Business Venturing, 25*(5), 439–448.

Ding, G. K. (2008). Sustainable construction: The role of environmental assessment tools. *Journal of Environmental Management, 86*(3), 451–464.

Hassan, A. S., Laul, A., Shah, K., Adebayo, A., Ebohon, O. J., Irurah, D. K., Rwelamila, P. D., ... John, V. M. (2002). In WSSD (Ed.), *Agenda 21 for sustainable construction in developing countries*. Pretoria, South Africa: CSIR Building and Construction Technology.

Holmes, J., & Hudson, G. (2000). An evaluation of the objectives of the BREEAM scheme for offices: A local case study. In *Proceedings of cutting edge 2000*. London: RICS Research Foundation, RICS.

Oke, A., Aigbavboa, C., & Ndou, M. (2018). Promoting sustainable construction through ecological economics. In *FIG Congress 2018 Embracing Smart World where the Continents Connect: Enhancing the Geospatial Maturity of Societies*, May 6–11, Turkey.

Oke, A. E., Aigbavboa, C. O., Stephen, S. S., & Thwala, W. D. (2021). *Sustainable construction in the era of the fourth industrial revolution*. London and New York, NY: Taylor and Francis Group. doi:10.1201/9781003179849-1

Ruževicius, J. (2010). Ecological footprint as an indicator of sustainable development. *Economics and Management, 2*(16), 711–718.

Windapo, A. O. (2014). Examination of green building drivers in the South African construction industry: Economics versus ecology. *Sustainability, 6*(9), 6088–6106.

Chapter 6

Grid Computing for Sustainable Infrastructure Management

Abstract

The interaction of systems through a designated control channel has improved communication, efficiency, management, storage, processing, etc. across several industries. The construction industry is an industry that thrives on a well-planned workflow rhythm; a change in the environmental dynamism will either have a positive or negative impact on the output of the project planned for execution. More so, raising the need for effective collaboration through workflow and project planning, grid application in construction facilitates the relationship between the project reality and the end users, all with the aim of improving resources and value management. However, decentralisation of close-domain control can cause uncertainty and incompleteness of data. And this can be a big factor, especially when a complex project is being executed.

Keywords: Computational infrastructure; construction software; construction systems; decentralisation; grid construction; sustainable construction

Introduction

The rapid increase in the advancement of software and the speed of hardware within the last few decades has resulted in the growth of commodity computing and network performance. This has made it possible to build high-performance computing systems at a very low cost. These high-performance systems, also known as clusters, can be used across several application domains to tackle resource-intensive challenges, enabling thorough simulations, experimentation, extensive data sharing and intensive collaboration of experimental activities and results analysis across the globe. In addition, all these complex operations can be conducted simultaneously, in real-time, and globally. On such a large scale of operation, many problems and challenges are certain to arise in the collaboration and integration of massive amounts of data and information across diverse

A Digital Path to Sustainable Infrastructure Management, 57–66
Copyright © 2024 Ayodeji E. Oke and Seyi S. Stephen
Published under exclusive licence by Emerald Publishing Limited
doi:10.1108/978-1-83797-703-120241006

organisations and administrations. Given this, a programme known as eScience was developed to facilitate collaborative research using computational infrastructure (Hey & Trefethwn, 2002). Below is an example of a typical eScience scenario in Fig. 1.

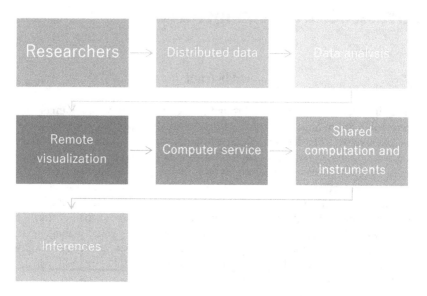

Fig. 1.   Showing a Typical eScience Scenario.

Data that are being computed and generated simultaneously within an eScience programme are massive and inherently distributed. So many issues arise, such as the security of data, management of access, distribution of information, processing of large computational data and long-term storage. This is where grid computing (GC) comes in; it integrates the distribution of wide-area resources such as storage servers, high-speed networks, databases, clusters and supercomputers; a massive computational infrastructure can be innovated to harness all the resources to form a grid infrastructure. This is similar to the framework of the electricity grid used in cities, which have the property of supplying services that are dependable, pervasive, consistent and transparent, regardless of the origin (Berman & Fox, 2003; Foster, Kesselman, Nick, & Tuecke, 2002; Parashar & Lee, 2005).

With regards to GC, a grid can be described as a structure that uses protocols and interfaces to manage and organise highly distributed services and resources across different domains to provide high-quality service (Foster et al., 2002). One of the most important qualities a grid must have is simplicity for the sake of usability. A grid should be able to manage large arrays of heterogeneous and connected information and provide a diverse combination of resources while allowing for different forms of sharing capabilities. According to Joseph, Ernest, and Fellenstein (2004), GC makes seamless remote computing available via very high-performance, tightly secure and highly scalable technologies.

GC in Today's World

GC is an invaluable infrastructure in large-scale resource sharing and in the integration of distributed systems in today's world (Foster et al., 2002). Distributed operations can utilise the benefits of GC, which benefits include information services, security, data transfer, resource management, workflow management, etc.

On the user's end of GC, several works on a global scale have developed many software and systems for seamless interaction within the grid environment. Grid middle-wares are useful to provide uniform access and smooth computing ability to all the necessary resources and information available in the grid environment and database. Examples of such resources include Globus and Gridbus. Globus was developed in the United States by scientists at Argonne National Laboratory and the University of Southern California. Gridbus was developed by researchers at the University of Melbourne in Australia. Globus and Gridbus are complementary in functionality for grid application and are meant to be used collectively. While Globus was built to provide core grid services, Gridbus was more for the user end, and it provides utility computing models for Grid resources management.

Over the years, different workflow techniques have been proposed and thus implemented into workflow management systems. However, workflow in a grid environment comes with certain challenges, such as:

a. *Cross-domain*: In a grid workflow system where work activities cut across several organisations, there is no central management and administration. This decentralisation of control can cause uncertainty and incompleteness of data.
b. *Dynamism*: So many factors come to play in a grid environment. Considering that it also involves the factor of a great amount of time, computational and networking capabilities may vary greatly, limiting the accuracy of application performance prediction and real-time information resource update (Pandey et al., 2009).

In a study by Cao, Jarvis, Saini, and Nudd (2003), there was a presentation on a workflow management system referred to as GridFlow. This GridFlow incorporates the combination of sub-local and global grid workflow management scheduling as presented by a user portal. At the global grid level, there is the existence of an agent-based Grid resource management system which is harnessed to provide the functions of simulation, execution and monitoring of workflow provided. At the local scale, an existing performance prediction-based task scheduling system is harnessed to provide sub-workflow scheduling and conflict management. The Grid system in this example is very dynamic and provides a comprehensive and immersive facility to manage a project from simulation, execution and monitoring at the managerial level to workflow monitoring, task scheduling and conflict resolution at the micro-scale.

In this example, new problems of workflow management are taken care of by using a fuzzy timing technique in a dynamic and cross-domain grid system (Murata, 1996). Fuzzy timestamps are used to represent workflow or task execution times. When conflicts occur, these fuzzy timestamps are calculated using fuzzy enabling times and combined possibility distributions. Using a case study to compare results, the researchers proved that fuzzy concepts can be feasibly used to manage multi-site scheduling in a grid environment. This shows beyond a doubt that grid management at a global scale and local scale can be integrated to work in tandem and utilised to optimise workflow efficiency and effectiveness.

How Does GC Work in Construction?

GC is a massive technological innovation. It involves the integration of large amounts of databases, computers, scientific instruments and networks into a collaborative and extensive framework. The aim is to achieve an immersive consolidation of large amounts of cross-organisational data and/or computing resources.

GC involves the sharing of organisational data across organisational boundaries. This operation carries a high risk as it requires high security. With this risk, GC, grid application management and grid deployment have very complex systems. Furthermore, in a grid system, there is the existence of a systematic structure that enables the integration of many frameworks in networks, databases, data (and big data), automation, etc. managed and structured by several organisations across disciplines. These systematic structures can be introduced from the onset of construction and reviewed throughout the stages of project delivery. In this, construction operations are enhanced through connected devices, but inadequacy in skills or operations can be fatal to the construction process irrespective of the time it was introduced (Jacob, Brown, Fukul, & Trivedi, 2005).

Grid is focused on solving problems arising due to massive collaborative research and facilitating the effectiveness of large-scale collaborative operations. GC among other things helps by:

- Enhancing distributed management systems while maintaining full control over locally managed resources.
- Enhancing the global access to data securely and solving problems related to data access patterns.
- Improving the productivity of researchers by providing them with a massive database of distributed information and facilities in a user-friendly format (Jacob et al., 2005).

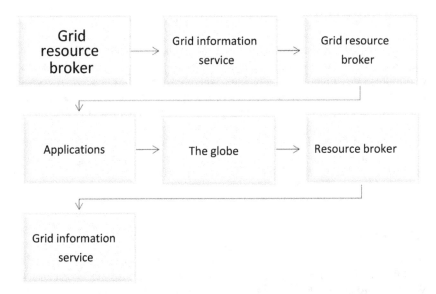

Fig. 2.   Example of a Scalable and High-Level View of a Grid
Framework.

Fig. 2 is an example of a scalable and high-level view of a grid framework. In this example, all grid resources are identified and registered within grid information services. When the global users submit an application requirement, the resource broker queries the information services, matches the required information of the different applications and schedules the execution of the application jobs based on these resources. The resource broker also monitors the processing and execution until completion. Such an operation like this runs on numerous requirements and would involve the inclusion of services such as security, directory, information, resource allocation, execution management, scheduling, application development and resource aggregation. Grid middleware is software tools that are incorporated into the grid structure to provide these extra requirements and functionalities.

The nature of the entire grid framework and the operation of systemising it produces a widely heterogeneous experience due to the vast range of hardware and software technologies engaged all at once in the system. In addition to this, information across the grid originates from diverse political, geographical and administrative demography across the world. It is so dynamic that it is unpredictable. The development of grid middleware is tasked to solve a majority of these issues (Baker, Buyya, & Laforenza, 2002).

This has resulted in the formulation of virtual organisations (VO), an endeavour that involves the collaboration of different organisations around the globe, working together to achieve a mutual objective by sharing necessary resources. Within a VO, certain rules are defined regarding the accessibility of resources that are already pre-defined. Depending on the objectives of the VO, different participants are granted different levels of urgency and priority and resource accessibility (Foster et al., 2002). Aside from the VO, another form of grid architecture involves a framework where resource consumers or users select resources based on their respective requirements, the price of the resource and the quality of service expected from resource providers. The resource providers or owners compete amongst themselves to supply the user best. The quality of service requested by the user is enforced by service level agreements (SLAs), regulating the interaction between provider and user and penalising violation of agreements. Users can indicate their expected quality-of-service deadlines and maximum price expected.

GC Devices

In the GC community, there are a limited amount of applications that address workflow circumstances. One of the earliest works currently no longer in use is WebFlow (Bhatia et al., 1997), which created computing applications of very high performance using a visual programming paradigm. Later, the common component architecture (CCA) was developed together with its XML implementation (Gannon et al., 2002) for grid programming. To be able to combine existing code with meta-programs without enacting changes to the code, Symphony was developed (Lorch & Kafura, 2002). For the specification of components within the grid environment and performance optimisation and implementation selection, Component XML (CXML) was developed for use in component-based grid applications. Other XML-based grid applications for accelerated strategic computing initiatives (ASCI) have been developed. Furthermore, the integration of Web Services protocols with GC resulted in the creation of web services flow language (WSFL) which can be utilised for grid workflow language (Leymann, 2001). Condor and UNICORE are also alternative grid applications that function under conditional infrastructures.

In a grid infrastructure, the grid computation is expected to support certain capabilities as described below (Salvadori, Gehrke, Oliveira, Campos, & Sausen, 2013):

- Composition of distributed applications using diverse software components including legacy programmes,
- Storing remotely in terms of replication of data sets,
- Discovery of suitable computational resources,
- Data sets discovery and publication in respect to global logical name and catalogued in attributes,
- Firm security in terms of access authorisation and uniform authentication,
- Data and computational resource as it relates to uniform access to remote resources,
- Submission, monitoring and steering of jobs execution,

- General accessibility to service and access costs,
- Accountability and reading (metring) of resource usage within a particular space and time,
- Uniform or aggregate distribution of services (jobs),
- Transferring of data/code across platforms and resources, and
- Enforcement of quality of service requirements.

Characteristics of GC

- *Large scale*: at such a large scale of grid functionality, and with grid inherently having as a defining characteristic the high potential for more and more increase in scale, a potential problem can be foreseen. Can the grid performance be maintained without degradation? As grid functions with high and powerful hardware and software, there is the need to continuously upgrade the capacity of the technologies used as this is critical to the continuity of GC.
- *Decentralisation*: as grid spans across the globe, information is highly decentralised, grid resources are remote from each other and grid is highly demanding on collection, database and organising.
- *Heterogeneity*: grid is the core of a system that is highly diverse and heterogeneous. A grid consists of several hardware and software resources, different forms and formats of scientific instruments, data and files, digital organisers, software components and programs, display devices, computers and supercomputers and networks. Yet, all these must be made to function collaboratively and seamlessly to grant a simple user access at a global scale.
- *Sharing capabilities*: in a grid, sharing is critical. Many grid data, information and resources belong to certain organisations that must allow access by other organisations (users). Grid must be well equipped to facilitate the sharing of different combination of data at a global scale in different file and software formats.
- *Decentralisation of administration*: in a grid, there already is the inherent challenge of network security. To make this even more cumbersome, different organisations in the grid have different policies and security administrations, which one must navigate before they can access the resources of that organisation. In a grid, there is no central administration and users have to deal with multiple and often inconvenient systems.
- *Consolidation and coordination of resources*: in a grid system, aggregated computing capabilities are paramount, and this can only be achieved by organised and meticulous integration of resources into the grid system.
- *Fabric layer*: resource types such as code repository, compute, storage and network resource are provided by the grid. These operations are only possible by existing fabric components such as local resource managers.
- *Connectivity layer*: this involves the core authentication and communication protocols of a grid system. The grid security infrastructure is always present in all grid transactions to ensure easy and secure network transactions.

- *Collective layer*: interactions across different resources and directories are facilitated in grid. Monitoring and Discovery Services (MDS) is an example of a grid service that provides monitoring and discovery of VO resources.
- *Application layer*: This is the layer of software that the user engages. It consists of applications that were developed on top of the grid protocols and APIs, and that can operate in the VO environment (Iosup & Epema, 2010).

Challenges of GC

GC presents myriad advantages and possibilities. However, it has its own problems and challenges as well. If these challenges are resolved, grid will truly attain its full capabilities, potential and functionalities.

- *Diverse standards*: GC involves various and diverse standards due to high heterogeneity. Different operating systems such as Linux, My SQL and Apache use UDDI, SOAP, XML, WWW and WSRF standards. Yet, the same computer can run on only one operating system at a time. Oracle 10g enterprise does not adopt the WSRF standard, and IBM developed J2EE grid middleware. A grid has the main challenge of dealing with the demand to coordinate across differing standards, at a large scale.
- *Distributed and GC*: the aim of grid is to make access to scientific data and repositories, experimental facilities and computing power as easily accessible as distributed information on the free web. Yet, grid is a lot more complicated than the free web, consisting dynamic VO, resource sharing and peer to peer computing.
- *Inadequate grid software*: there are not currently a lot of software that are grid-enabled. Copyright issues and source code licence issues arise for the sparse software available. As it is now, more developers need to dedicate time to developing grid-enabled software.
- *Resource sharing*: the cross-domain quality of grid poses the challenge of sharing large resources across different sites, software and domains within VOs.
- *Complexity of software development*: grid programming uses XML, JAVA, WSDD, WSDL, UDDI, WSRF and other services. Software developers must be very skilled in order to develop functionally for such a complex system (Jin, 2005).

Conclusion

In recent years, GC has rapidly developed into a mainstream utility for the distribution and sharing of large-scale resources across several systems integrations for a particular target (Cao et al., 2003). The innovative GridFlow structure presented by Cao et al. (2003) proves that it is possible to integrate GC at a global scale and local scale to efficiently manage operations synchronously. Since the construction industry is a major player in global economic development, GC can aid the construction process. However, the challenges that come with its adoption can be detrimental to a project's success, yet its benefits cannot be neglected due to a few problems.

References

Baker, F., Buyya, R., & Laforenza, D. (2002). Grids and grid technologies for wide-area distributed computing. *International Journal of Software: Practice and Experience (SPE)*, *32*(15), 1437–1466.

Berman, G., & Fox, A. (2003). In T. Hey (Ed.), *Grid computing: Making the global infrastructure a reality*. New York, NY: Wiley Press.

Bhatia, D., Burzevski, V., Camuseva, M., Fox, G., Furmanski, W., & Premchandran, G. (1997). WebFlow – A visual programming paradigm for Web/Java based coarse grain distributed computing. *Concurrency: Practice and Experience*, *9*(6), 555–577.

Cao, J., Jarvis, S. A., Saini, S., & Nudd, G. R. (2003). Gridflow: Workflow management for grid computing. In *CCGrid 2003. 3rd Institute of Electrical and Electronics Engineers (IEEE)/Association of Computing Machinery (ACM) International Symposium on Cluster Computing and the Grid, 2003. Proceedings* (pp. 198–205). Institute of Electrical and Electronics Engineers (IEEE).

Foster, I., Kesselman, C., Nick, J. M., & Tuecke, S. (2002). Grid services for distributed system integration. *Institute of Electrical and Electronics Engineers (IEEE) Computer*, *35*(6), 37–46.

Gannon, D., Balasubramanian, J., Bramley, R., Diwan, S., Govindaraju, M., Krishnan, S., & Slominski, A. (2002). *Building applications from a web service based component architecture*. Retrieved from https://www.cs.uoregon.edu/research/paracomp/papers/cca_cpe04/html/node3.html

Hey, T., & Trefethwn, A. E. (2002). The UK e-science core programme and the grid. In P. M. A. Sloot, A. G. Hoekstra, C. J. K. Tan, & J. J. Dongarra (Eds.), *Computational Science-ICCS 2002. Lecture Notes in Computer Science* (Vol. 2329). Berlin, Heidelberg: Springer. doi:10.1007/3-540-46043-8_1

Iosup, A., & Epema, D. (2010). Grid computing workloads. *Institute of Electrical and Electronics Engineers (IEEE) Internet Computing*, *15*(2), 19–26.

Jacob, B., Brown, M., Fukul, K., & Trivedi, N. (2005). *Introduction to grid computing*. Retrieved from https://www.uettaxila.edu.pk

Jin, H. (2005). Challenges of grid computing. In W. Fan, Z. Wu, & J. Yang (Eds.), *Advances in web-age information management. Lecture Notes in Computer Science* (Vol. 3739). Berlin, Heidelberg: Springer. doi:10.1007/11563952_3

Joseph, J., Ernest, M., & Fellenstein, C. (2004). Evolution of grid computing architecture and grid adoption models. *International Business Machine (IBM) Systems Journal*, *43*(4), 624–645.

Leymann, F. (2001). *Web Services Flow Language (WSFL 1.0)*. Retrieved from https://www.xml.coverpages.org

Lorch, M., & Kafura, D. (2002). Symphony – A Java-based composition and manipulation framework for computational grids. In *Proceedings of 2nd Institute of Electrical and Electronics Engineers (IEEE)/Association of Computing Machinery (ACM) International Symposium on Cluster Computing and the Grid*, Berlin, Germany (pp. 136–143).

Murata, T. (1996). Temporal uncertainty and fuzzy-timing high-level Petri nets. In J. Billington & W. Reisig (Eds.), *Application and theory of Petri nets 1996. ICATPN. Lecture Notes in Computer Science* (Vol. 1091). Berlin, Heidelberg: Springer. doi: 10.1007/3-540-61363-3_2

Pandey, S., Voorsluys, W., Rahman, M., Buyya, R., Dobson, J. E., & Chiu, K. (2009). A grid workflow environment for brain imaging analysis on distributed systems. *Concurrency and Computation: Practice and Experience, 21*(16), 2118–2139.

Parashar, M., & Lee, C. A. (2005). Grid computing: Introduction and overview. *Proceedings of the Institute of Electrical and Electronics Engineers (IEEE) Systems Journal, Special Issue on Grid Computing, 93*(3), 479–484.

Salvadori, F., Gehrke, C., Oliveira, A. C., Campos, M., & Sausen, P. S. (2013). Smart grid infrastructure using a hybrid network architecture. *Institute of Electrical and Electronics Engineers (IEEE) Transactions on Smart Grid, 4*(3), 1630–1639.

Chapter 7

Mobile Cloud Computing for Sustainable Infrastructure Management

Abstract

Mobile computing enables mobile devices to boost restricted resources, and this further includes processing, storage space and battery freedom with the help of cloud facilities. Cloud computing (CC) enables users to obtain admission to energy from another location, providing movement, and enabling common data admission. This chapter is tailored towards responding to a variety of the main challenges of the construction industry with the help of utilising mobile cloud solutions and services. The main benefits of embracing CC largely centred on resources which are expressed in cost reduction, system mobility, system flexibility and system maintenance, while the threats are information protection, individual accessibility, governing conformity, data location, accessibility and also disaster recuperation. This chapter provided necessary solutions to the main threats in the construction industry in terms of design, materials, finance, management and knowledge with the application of mobile cloud computing.

Keywords: Cloud computing; construction industry; construction mobility; information management; mobile computing; sustainable construction innovation

Introduction

Construction information management has substantially gained breakthroughs in information through the interaction of modern technologies by raising the rate of information, boosting the effectiveness and efficiency of communication in construction (Chen & Kamara, 2007). These breakthroughs are also visible in terms of improved network rates across connected systems, efficient mobile applications and on-site monitoring made possible through the application.

Building sites are information-extensive atmospheres where real building construction procedures and tasks are executed. Different building and construction workers in the area require huge quantities of details varying from jobs

A Digital Path to Sustainable Infrastructure Management, 67–74

Copyright © 2024 Ayodeji E. Oke and Seyi S. Stephen

Published under exclusive licence by Emerald Publishing Limited

doi:10.1108/978-1-83797-703-120241007

to executing a particular scheduled programme of work. So, to check out and create efficient techniques for on-site details administration, every factor must be considered and well balanced with on-site building details which can come in the form of classifications.

The building and construction market is a fragmented industry. Several stakeholders and events in the industry enable several collaborations of professionals to efficiently implement and execute tasks. This market has constantly experienced difficulties in financial resources, credibility, efficiency and so on. To solve this, the construction industry has undergone several technological changes concerning incorporating sustainability into its process and applying new associated innovations such as building information modelling (BIM), mobile cloud computing (MCC), artificial intelligence (AI), virtual reality (VR), robotics, etc.; and this has systematically altered the regular life cost cycle of projects (Silverio, Renukappa, Sresh, & Donastorg, 2017).

Also, the incorporation of new monitoring devices as well as other contemporary methods into the built industry has improved project efficiency, interaction and delivery over time. Using a popular example, smartphones inculcated into the building and construction field can be utilised to address several primary obstacles discovered across the stages of project planning, execution and even management. Since MCC is the broader application of these mobile devices in construction, and its popularity gaining overtime incessantly over the years, it is no doubt the construction industry will experience much more advanced technological practices, and they will in turn push the industry to the summit more than the one presently witnessed.

Mobile Computing (MC) in Construction

MC tends to widen information across websites from that of the workplace to the project site within convenience. Real-time information concerning the project can be easily passed through a designated medium to all participants on a project with little or no hassle whatsoever. Also, through the integration of computerised networks, MC has the prospective to raise the efficient use of information technology (IT) in a construction firm where it is incorporated either as the main system or as an alternative means of operation.

In the study by Chen and Kamara (2011), the researchers stated that mobile computer innovations can be used to address specific issues as well as other related challenges in construction from the onset of the project to its completion. These applications include supervision, monitoring, positioning system, estimating, designs and so on.

Mobile computer technologies have been executed in several building procedures. Rebolj, Babič, Magdič, Podbreznik, and Pšunder (2008) created a computerised building task surveillance system based upon a mobile computer sustained interaction setting. Also, Dong, Maher, Kim, and GuWang (2009) reviewed a straight tabletop interface that integrates mobile computer and cordless interaction to assist in synchronous building website to workplace cooperation for an enhanced building administration. Other functionalities can be referenced in terms of the safety and security of the cordless network, computer-aided design (CAD) information visu-alisation on smartphones and real-time navigating support group (Strachan & Stephenson, 2009).

Cloud Computing (CC)

The principle of CC was initially presented in 2004 (Vouk, 2008). It has been defined by different specialists, especially in the business sector and scholastic areas with various points of view and perspectives. In a study by Silverio et al. (2017), it was defined as a model that enables balanced and expedient configu-rations between on-demand network access and a shared pool of configurable computing resources regarding networking, service across servers, storing, applications and services that can be rapidly provisioned and released with minimal management effort or service provider interaction. CC additionally gives a healthy and balanced workplace that makes use of online computer innovation to decrease making use of numerous web servers, and computer systems, and thus improves the strive towards sustainability (Menken, 2012).

Benefits of MCC in Construction Management

The breakthroughs in economical mobile smart phones have improved wireless network move rates, renovations in mobile application efficiency, provide mobile computer modern technology with an effective prospective to boost on-site building and construction details monitoring. Nonetheless, in the past, using this new modern technology, it is essential to recognise the functions of mobile computer even as information concerning construction workers and other on-site details are paramount to its adoption and application in construction (Chen & Kamara, 2007).

Mobile computer can further be utilised to enhance the effectiveness of information interaction on construction site through an examined website setting. This and other significances have improved construction in terms of:

- Accessibility to project information,
- Keeping of records,
- Swift information conversion,
- Improve location identification,
- Resources allocation,
- Up-to-date inventory,
- Project execution,
- Enhanced construction operations, and
- Increase in performance and predictability (Cheng & Kumar, 2012; Oke, Aigbavboa, Stephen, & Thwala, 2021).

According to IT cloud survey conducted by International Data Corpora-tion, Cheng and Kumar (2012) examined previous study regarding the benefits of CC designs. The nature of the building and construction sector in relation to CC design was examined with major benefits identified in terms of building enhancements in regards to cost, mobility, versatility, maintenance and updating. Also, it was asserted that CC in construction helps in partnership among the parties involved, especially in regards to monitoring and dissemination of information. These benefits are further expatiated below.

Cost Reduction: The standard way of IT distribution developed varies from one CC design to another. Generally, this variation is as a result of the utility-based prices of each design pertaining to functionality and type. Many architectural engineering and construction (AEC) firms are now embracing CC into their operations; hence, there has been reduction in costly errors (design, plan, and build) on project sites. Even with some of these AEC firms being middle-sized ventures with sizeable number of workers, efficiency is expected within the available resources and CC comes into the fray with operations that requires sizeable input, and this in turn helps to maintain and reduce project budget as well as project completion duration (Cheng & Kumar, 2012).

System Mobility: In a CC environment, systems and programs run in the cloud. This implies that different users can access the exact same information from various places and run successful operations computationally through applications which function to operate in architectural designs, evaluation and structural analysis via network-enabled tools such as smart phones or desktop computers (Silverio et al., 2017).

System Flexibility: The degree of IT required for project process in order to carry out different tasks differs throughout its life process, and this is basically why cloud-based sources are practical in design in order to cater for differences, variations and exemptions during project execution. In so much that it is mobile across different templates, mobility and flexibility of MCC comes into function in relation to prices, operations, process, time, etc. (Silverio et al., 2017).

Challenges in the Adoption of MCC in Sustainable Construction

MCC is considered to have its share of threats both to the project and the user. In Brender and Markov (2013), information insecurity, user inaccessibility, governing conformity and loss of data have been touted as the major disadvantages of using MCC in construction presented along with other challenges in Table 1. A further concern has also been raised in terms of awareness in terms of its functionality since some professionals think that it constitutes a major threat to a project more than the identified benefits provided.

Information security is one of the main issues in the adoption of cloud services; the presence of innovation and also the huge focus of information on the internet give an eye-catching target for cyberpunks (ENISA, 2009). Following Caroll, Der Merwe, and Kotze (2011), meeting with individuals in Southern Africa, information protection and user accessibility were taken into serious consideration among the major dangers. For a much better comprehension, it is needed to keep in mind that the refining of delicate information outdoors the firm properties

Table 1. Challenges in the Adoption of Mobile Cloud Computing (MCC).

Authors	Challenges in the Adoption of MCC
Brender and Markov (2013)	<ul><li>information insecurity</li><li>user inaccessibility</li><li>governing conformity</li><li>loss of data</li><li>level of awareness</li></ul>
Caroll et al. (2011)	<ul><li>information exposure</li><li>subject to hacking</li><li>user interaction</li></ul>

bypasses the safety embraced by the interior IT division. The developed remedy to this issue is to utilise the concept of the very least benefit, which advises granting individuals or procedures the very least opportunities as well as sources in the fastest period needed to complete a certain task (Marinescu, 2018).

MCC as a Solution to the Challenge of Sustainable Construction

MCC brings all the advantages and dangers of cloud computer to smart phones, therefore supplying information to its users. This section takes a look at how MCC tends to sustain the construction industry in the drives towards green building. The challenges to address are design, materials, finance, management and knowledge.

Solution for Design Obstacles: following Proverbs, Holt, and Cheok (2000), over-specification is among the major issues related to design. As a result of over-specification, some structures are located to have unneeded attributes and locations. Nonetheless, there are currently more modern technologies connected to areas of buildings created such as BIM and CAD that provides developers with a quicker and faster-developed cycle. With the execution of innovations such as BIM as well as CAD in today's sector, a lot of created interactions and modifications will occur throughout the building execution, which is among the primary factors for design-related mistakes. BIM as an example brings the suggestion of combining all designs into one version with the aim of enhancing construction efficiency.

Services for Material-Related Difficulties: the building sector is faced with the absence of eco-friendly products that help sustain the environment. In some cases where these products or materials are available, they are sometimes wasted due to inadequate knowledge of the functions of these materials or products, inadequate supervision, inadequate skills to harness their potential, etc. These barriers have direct influences on the successful adoption of sustainable concepts into construction. However, the major remedy for these obstacles is to supply electronic management of the whole product life process, which is from production to other supply chain management aided by the application of CC. Today, mobile phones such as tablet computers can give common remedies to remove paper products dealing with procedures.

Options for Economic Obstacles: economic difficulties have been constantly experienced in the building sector. But lately, with the improved adoption of brand-new lasting advancement techniques, individuals are stressed over boosted financial investment prices and lengthy repayment durations. Ayarkwa, Agyekum, and Adinyira (2011) from a monetary point of view, CC can increase economic status following task demands, which assists to lower setbacks in building projects; nonetheless, reduction in setbacks reductions will assist in removing common monetary obstacles in building tasks, as well as monetary elements connected to sustainability.

Remedies for Monitoring Difficulties: task monitoring consists of elements related to building such as efficiency, job setting up and phases of the procedure. Shehu and Akintoye (2010) determined the primary obstacles to the effective exercise of job monitoring in the UK building industry, and gave that a few of the major obstacles are hold-ups in task distribution, absence of understanding to examine dangers and absence of cross-functional interaction. MCC enables the usage of monitoring devices in the field; for that reason, supervisors can surely incorporate these works into their task-monitoring techniques.

Options for Understanding Difficulties: the knowledge-related obstacles present in the building sector are generally associated with the absence of abilities or technological understanding needed for particular jobs on the task. Häkkinen and Belloni (2011) expressed concern over the absence of understanding and lasting details in construction jobs, and highlighted how MCC can aid these regards in working towards a sustainable construction industry. Further study by Ayarkwa et al. (2011) gave some of the barriers connected to expertise and understanding as the absence of specialist expertise, absence of client recognition, absence of recognition of rate of passion, lack of knowledge/misunderstanding of sustainability and illiteracy. Rather than being limited or confined to a particular understanding of challenges in construction, MCC provides alternatives in assessment, review, connectivity and decision-making.

Conclusions

MCC exists as a mobile innovation that is versatile and easy to manage. It relieves source restrictions on mobile phones by boosting storage space, power and application. With significant innovations in firms like Google, Amazon, Apple, etc. serving as shadow providers, we can anticipate these businesses to make substantial and constant initiatives to boost information protection. By addressing the advantages and threats of MCC, create, products, financing, monitoring and understanding were identified as significant difficulties in the construction market. Functionalities brought about in terms of accessibility and capacity made easier with the inclusion of MCC in construction practice, the industry can produce and incorporate brand-new devices to maximise various facets of construction irrespective of the size or the nature of the project.

References

Ayarkwa, J., Agyekum, K., & Adinyira, E. (2011). Barriers to sustainable implementation of lean construction in the Ghanaian building industry. In *Paper presented at the Sixth Built Environment Conference*, Johannesburg, South Africa, July 31–August 2, 2011 (p. 67).

Brender, N., & Markov, I. (2013). Risk perception and risk management in cloud computing: Results from a case study of Swiss companies. *International Journal of Information Management, 33*(5), 726–733.

Caroll, M., Der Merwe, A. V., & Kotze, P. (2011). *Secure cloud computing: Benefits, risks and controls.* Retrieved from https://www.ieeexlore.ieee.org

Cheng, J. C., & Kumar, B. (2012). Mobile and pervasive computing in construction. *Cloud Computing Support for Construction Collaboration, 1*(1), 237–254. doi:10.1002/9781118422281.Ch12

Chen, Y., & Kamara, J. M. (2007). Using mobile computing for construction site information management. *Engineering Construction and Architectural Management, 15*(1), 7–20.

Chen, Y., & Kamara, J. M. (2011). A framework for using mobile computing for information management on construction sites. *Automation in Construction, 20*(7), 7776–7881.

Dong, M. L., Maher, M., Kim, J., & GuWang, N. X. (2009). Construction defect management using a telematic digital workbench. *Automation in Construction, 18*(6), 814–824.

European Network and Information Security Agency (ENISA). (2009). *Cloud computing: Benefits, risks and recommendations for information security.* Retrieved from https://www.enisa.europa.eu

Häkkinen, T., & Belloni, K. (2011). Barriers and drivers for sustainable building. *Building Research & Information, 39*(3), 239–255.

Marinescu, D. C. (2018). Cloud security. *Cloud Computing Theory and Practice, 5*(1), 405–437. doi:10.1016/B978-0-12-812810-7.00015-7

Menken, I. (2012). *An introduction to cloud computing.* Brisbane: Emereo Publishing.

Oke, A. E., Aigbavboa, C. O., Stephen, S. S., & Thwala, W. D. (2021). *Sustainable construction in the era of the fourth industrial revolution.* London, New York: Taylor and Francis Group. doi:10.1201/9781003179849-1

Proverbs, D. G., Holt, G. D., & Cheok, H. Y. (2000). Construction industry problems: The views of UK construction directors. In A. Akintoye (Ed.), 16th Annual ARCOM Conference, 6-8 September 2000, Glasgow Caledonian University. *Association of Researchers in Construction Management, 1*(2), 73–81.

Rebolj, D., Babič, N., Magdič, A., Podbreznik, P., & Pšunder, M. (2008). Automated construction activity monitoring system. *Advanced Engineering Informatics, 22*(4), 493–503.

Shehu, Z., & Akintoye, A. (2010). Major challenges to the successful implementation and practice of programme management in the construction environment: A critical analysis. *International Journal of Project Management, 28*(1), 26–39.

Silverio, M., Renukappa, S., Sresh, S., & Donastorg, A. (2017). Mobile computing in the construction industry: Main challenges and solutions. In *Springer proceedings in business and economics.* Springer Cham. doi:10.1007/978-3-319-43434_8

Strachan, R., & Stephenson, P. (2009). Futuristic construction communication infrastructures: Secure and safe with no wires, special issue next generation construction IT: Technology foresight, future studies, road mapping, and scenario planning. *Journal of Information Technology in Construction*, *14*(2), 526–539.

Vouk, M. A. (2008). Cloud computing – Issues, research and implementations. *Institute of Electrical and Electronics Engineers (IEEE)*, *1*(1), 31–40.

Chapter 8

Smart Contract for Sustainable Infrastructure Management

Abstract

Today, sustainability is considered a high priority; and it is on the agenda for major corporations. It has experienced an increase due to the demands of the customers, thereby pressuring corporations to act in more sustainable ways to stay relevant and competitive. One industry that is experiencing an increased request to act sustainably is the construction industry. The construction industry differs quite a lot from other industries since it is project-based and built on temporary relationships. Subcontractors are temporarily engaged in the projects, often by a main contractor, to perform tasks in which they are specialised. The subcontractors additionally engage their respective subcontractors. This makes it harder to control and ensure that all involved actors are acting sustainably due to the multiple tiers of contractors and the complex nature of the projects. A technology that recently has had the attention of construction professionals is blockchain technology, which is built on smart contracts. It can be described as a shared, distributed ledger technology, which was created as an enabler for the cryptocurrency Bitcoin. The technology has, in recent years, been widely discussed as a potential business enhancer. It can, for example, provide immutable record-keeping, enables the usage of smart contracts and enhance transparency within the network, which is deemed valuable to the construction industry's push towards sustainability. The smart contracts technology has the potential to disrupt current business practices and decrease the required amounts of trust needed in business relationships.

Keywords: Blockchain technology; construction digitalisation; crypto-currencies; digitalised contract; smart contract; sustainable construction

A Digital Path to Sustainable Infrastructure Management, 75–83
Copyright © 2024 Ayodeji E. Oke and Seyi S. Stephen
Published under exclusive licence by Emerald Publishing Limited
doi:10.1108/978-1-83797-703-120241008

Introduction

Sustainability in construction has been stressed over time as the solutions to limitations experienced from the onset of construction to the extent of project delivery. Not only does the concept of sustainability involve benefits to the environment, but it also encompasses positive contributions to the social, physical and economic aspect of construction, and the entire nation as a whole (Cardeira, 2015). To establish the practices involved in sustainable construction, there have been introductions of concepts that include: smart contracts, automation across systems, cloud computing, aerial-enabled systems, etc. All these concepts are directed towards bringing value across the several sections of construction design, planning and executions within that which are sustainable, efficient and progressive in the standard and whole life cycle.

The construction industry is experiencing increasing sustainability awareness within its projects. This includes materials that have less impact on the environment which are fairly produced, as well as labour conditions and other social aspects during actual construction (Presley & Meade, 2010). The construction industry is a long-chain industry and this makes it challenging. For example, the main contractors are the actors who have overall responsibilities for construction, thus placing them in a position where they are the ones responsible for realising the sustainability demands. The main contractor has a coordinating role in construction projects as well as performing tasks during construction. However, it is highly unusual that they possess all the skills required for the entire project, which is one of the reasons why they engage subcontractors. The subcontractors themselves also engage other subcontractors (depending on the nature, size and type of project) to support their operations. This creates a complex chain of several tiers of subcontractors within the construction project where the monitoring and control of actors are thus challenging and resources demanding tasks (Sears, Sears, Clough, Rounds, & Segner, 2015).

New technologies that have emerged throughout time have changed the world, how to run businesses, and the way we live our lives. Equal to what electricity did for society at that time, network-based digitalisation is the driving force today for both businesses and private lives (Vogelsang, 2010). One technology that is widely discussed as a potential enhancer of business and everyday life is smart contract technology. Smart contract today is mostly associated with cryptocurrencies, especially Bitcoin. As stated by Gupta (2017), the technology was created as an enabler for Bitcoin and has had its biggest area of usage within cryptocurrencies so far. The technology has, however, been discussed to have beneficial features for other business practices as well.

The 'smart contract technology can be explained as a shared, distributed ledger technology that records transactions that are made within a network' (Gupta, 2017). The ledger is held by the nodes within the network, which are peer-to-peer and replicated against each other. Peer-to-peer replication can be described as a continuous synchronisation against all nodes within the network, at all times. This enables the use of a consensus-based model, where the true version of the ledger lies in the majority of the network members, compared to today where the ledger is often held by a central authority that is trusted to hold the ledger at a true state (Dhillon, Metcalf, & Hooper, 2017). This is referred to as the trust-based model. Smart contract technology enables transactions to be recorded and stored in an immutable way (Morabito, 2017). The main purpose of the smart contract technology, since it was developed as an enabler for the cryptocurrency Bitcoin, is to move the governance of the system from a central party to the distributed mass. This creates an assurance of a true ledger since the majority of the network otherwise needs to coordinate manipulation of the same record at the same time to make it pass through unnoticeable (Gupta, 2017). Even though smart contract technology was created as an enabler for Bitcoin, it has been widely discussed to be a technology that can be used in a business context when considered properly.

The smart contract setup can be designed so that all the actors within the network are visible to each other. This can enhance the transparency in the business network which enables the business relationships to not solely rely on trust. Smart contract technology can substitute this trust thanks to the immutability and visibility it provides, allowing the actors to trace the information (Dhillon et al., 2017). These characteristics of the smart contract technology may be the potential to enable a more sustainable environment for all actors within the network. Since there is a general demand within the construction industry to actively work towards 'a more fair and sustainable industry, exploring digitalisation in the construction industry, smart contracts in construction, application of smart contracts for sustainable development, the potentials and the barriers to the implementation of smart contracts in the construction' industry will propel the construction industry forward than ever imagined.

Digitalisation in Construction

The application of technology in arranging, formulating and executing contractual processes has become prevalent over the years due to the massive influx of technologically advanced practices engaged now in construction. Liu and Zhao (2014) in their study stated that many information technology applications are developed to improve contract management in construction. One such is the data warehouse which provides data access for references and decision-making at the appropriate time during the period of contract administration (Yih Chong, Balamuralithara, & Choy Chong, 2011). This type of technological application is useful for construction practitioners who are with or without limited legal knowledge to successfully carry out contract administration (Yih Chong et al., 2011). Contract change management (CCM) is an online collaborative tool for ensuring a smooth CCM process under the new engineering contract (NEC). Many construction professionals in the United Kingdom acknowledged the benefits of the CCM in supporting the contract process as it allows them to notify each other as soon as certain conditions become apparent, which may lead to project changes at a later stage (Sun & Oza, 2010). Domashova, Pisarchik, and Lifar (2018) developed a technology using PHP 7.1 programming language and

MySQL 5.6 to detect overpriced public contracts promptly. Therefore, this prevents corrupt tendencies that can lead to 'disputes in construction' contracts.

The application of technology to support contractual arrangements in construction involves the promotion and application of smart contracts. According to Cardeira (2015), smart contracts are computer protocols that facilitate, verify or enforce the negotiation or performance of a contract, or that obviate the need for a contractual clause. Similarly, smart contracts are transactions that take place between verified parties and are executed by a computer code (Lamb, 2018). Smart contracts use blockchain technology. This technology enables digital information to be distributed without copying or alteration features (Wang, Wu, Wang, & Shou, 2017). In addition, transactions are grouped in blocks per time and then added to a block of chain that cannot be altered or hacked. This increases data security. In a contractual arrangement, parties can access the same information in the blockchain at any time throughout the project lifecycle (Wang et al., 2017). This eliminates the issue of lack of trust as no one party has more information than the other at a time. Smart contracts are embedded with digital currencies in the contract together with several conditions that have to be fulfiled before payment (Cardeira, 2015). In essence, the clauses in smart contracts are self-executing (Wang et al., 2017). In summary, the use of smart contracts can eliminate payment/cash flow issues, improve the efficiency of the contract administration process and elimination of trust concerns in the contractual arrangements in the construction industry.

Smart Contract

The foundation of smart contracts is embedded in the blockchain. Blockchain is a type of cryptocurrency system that enables transactions across interfaces among users (Laurence, 2017; Oke, Aigbavboa, Stephen, & Thwala, 2021). To further explanation of what blockchain entails, there are three main parts involved in its actualisation. These parts are blocks, chains and networks available to registered users for a particular execution within a specified time frame. Furthermore, blocks in the blockchain are linked together to form chains encored in networks through cryptographic hash centred towards validity and existence between an old (previous) and the parent blocks. This is explained in the game theory that enables competition between full nodes concerning finding the correct hash function and collecting subsequent rewards in tokens as in cryptocurrency (Laurence, 2017).

In addition, Laurence (2017) further stated that when the correct hash function is found, the block is then locked to the previous block in chronological order and is time-stamped by the hash created. The network is maintained by all nodes within the network. Laurence (2017) refers to the nodes that hold the ledgers as full nodes. Each of these nodes holds a complete record of all transactions made within the blockchain which creates the consensus the network is built upon. The full nodes secure the network since they generate the cryptographic codes that chain the blocks together, and that they hold the ledger that creates the peer-to-peer replication within the network. Within the cryptocurrency world, the full nodes are referred to as miners. These nodes are decentralised and operate all over the world. Anyone can operate a full node and is rewarded for it because of the difficulty and expense of running it. The reward depends on the network but is usually in the form of cryptocurrencies or a token.

Dhillon et al. (2017) state that blockchain technology is based on consensus, which aligns stakeholders who may commonly harbor mistrust. The single node does not need to trust another single node, but rather the network as a whole, creating consensus. In other words, it is a self-correcting and honest system that does not require any enforcement of the rules by a trusted third party.

Smart Contract in Today's World

A contract is an agreement that gives the involved parties a legally binding document that defines what rights and obligations are necessary cored on promoting long-term relationships, according to Morabito (2017). A contract has a certain intention and is voluntary to agree upon. A contract is only valid and enforceable, from the perspective of the law. Morabito (2017) states that not all contracts are required to be put in writing for it to be binding but it will protect the parties if, for example, there is a breach and the dispute needs to be settled by a court of law. The breach can be when one party does not live up to the agreed conditions upon performance that the contacts states. Some contracts are required to be put into writing to be irrevocable and binding. This can be selling or buying real estate, rental agreements, the financing of a leasing agreement or policies of home insurance.

The concept of contractual arrangement irrespective of the nature of the contract is subject to trust and expectancy. Ryan (2017) buttressed this by stating that business transaction is possible especially when there is a previous or current relationship (in trust) between the parties involved in the business transaction. It was further stated that smart contract offers trust, reliability and executions within the swiftest possible duration with little or no hassle especially when there is a corresponding setup for its execution. Furthermore, Mik (2017) and Morabito (2017) gave additional insight into what a smart contract is by stating its functionalities in coded computer distinctions where logic triggers further action concerning trust and management.

In a further study by Morabito (2017), it was opined that for the smart contract to function properly, it requires information that verifies the terms for the agreement to be executed. Some contracts require information outside the blockchain to perform by the set terms. This requires the need for links to external data that are trusted. There are two types of smart contracts: deterministic and non-deterministic. Deterministic contracts only require information available on the blockchain, i.e. no outside information is required. This makes that deterministic contracts can execute and work efficiently since it only requires the information available within the blockchain, i.e. no outside information, meaning that the network has enough information to execute the contract.

Non-deterministic contracts are smart contracts that need additional information that is not available within the blockchain network (Morabito, 2017). For these types of contracts, a trusted third party from outside the blockchain needs to be brought in to provide the information required to execute the contracts. As further stated by Morabito (2017), these third parties are called Oracles and are agreed upon by the contractual parties. The Oracle can be seen as an agent that is programmable to provide the smart contract with the information required. The Oracles only pass along the information that is required, making it efficient, secure and ensuring privacy. It can be seen that the data is pushed onto the blockchain by Oracle rather than being pulled into the smart contract.

Morabito (2017) continued that a smart contract can be used for, example for car rental. The Internet of Things (IoT) can enable the smart contract in terms that it unlocks the door of the car when an event has been triggered on the smart contract. Szabo (1997), who laid the foundation for smart contracts, states that a smart contract can be used to finance the purchase of a car. If the payments are not made in time, the car will not unlock the doors with the digital key the buyer has. Businesses that profit from running a platform as a trusted party, such as Airbnb, may be excessive in the future due to blockchains. Morabito (2017) concluded that by using IoT, a business model such as Airbnb's would get eliminated since a smart contract can carry out the sublet of an apartment with digital keys that only works for the time interval the tenant has paid for. These digital keys can be in the tenants' smartphones and only be used if all terms of the agreement are met.

Smart contracts have several areas of usage and are highly beneficial in many terms. Sklaroff (2017) states that since the contract is written entirely in code, the cost of ambiguities in the written text, judicial counselling and the drafting of the contract, is avoided. The risk for opportunistic behaviour is also mitigated since the potentially written interpretations of the terms are eliminated. Sklaroff (2017) further states that smart contracts are seen as a possible replacement for traditional contract law. This is expressed since the business can be negotiated without the need for laws and courts, terms negotiated on their own, and connect the smart contract directly to the parties' internal information systems to enforce the transactions. So regular business-to-business transactions can draw benefits from the technology. It is however of great importance to point out that smart contracts are not supposed to replace all semantic contracts. Smart contracts are most useful in areas such as routine transactions that are made frequently. Sklaroff (2017) further states that firms today see contractual flexibility as a crucial necessity for conducting business and smart contracts that fail to deliver the flexibility will be of limited usage.

Types of Smart Contracts

Smart contract mostly comes in two types, they are deterministic and non-deterministic smart contracts discussed below:

Deterministic contracts: these types of contract only require information that is available on the blockchain, i.e. no outside information is required. This means that deterministic contracts can execute and work efficiently since it only requires the information available within the blockchain, i.e. no outside information, meaning that the network has enough information to execute the contract.

Non-deterministic contracts: are smart contracts that need additional information that is not available within the blockchain network (Morabito, 2017). For these types of contracts, a trusted third party from outside the blockchain needs to be brought in to provide the information required to execute the contracts. As further discussed by Morabito (2017), these third parties are called Oracles and are agreed upon by the contractual parties. The Oracle can be seen as an agent that is programmable to provide the smart contract with the information required. The Oracles only pass along the information that is required, making it efficient, secure and ensures privacy.

Challenges of Implementing Smart Contract in the Construction Industry

In as much as many benefits are accustomed to the implementation of smart contract in construction, the listed below are some of the challenges facing its implementation and adoption in the construction industry:

- Inadequate awareness by the construction professionals and the clients (Cardeira, 2015),
- Blockchain technology is perceived to be at the early stage of development (Wang et al., 2017),
- Redundant attitude to embracing new technology (Cardeira, 2015),
- Elongated time, bandwidth, size in processing and implementation (Cardeira, 2015),
- Restriction to human negotiation and considerations in case of market price fluctuations (Wang et al., 2017),
- Inhibits construction professional's participation in contract process (Mason & Escott, 2018).

Benefits of Implementing Smart Contracts in the Construction Industry

- Wang et al. (2017) described the smart contract as an application of blockchain technology for maintaining optimal trust in the following ways. The first one is to eliminate payment and cash flow problems. This is possible due to the self-executing mechanism of the smart contract. As stated by Cardeira (2015), a smart contract is an efficient mechanism and process to hasten payments between clients and contractors, and subcontractors, to guide against insolvencies in the construction industry.

- The second one is to improve efficiency in the contract administration process, especially in terms of project duration, due to the automated and unambiguous process. Additionally, Mason and Escott (2018) stated that the use of smart contracts can reduce the amount of paperwork in contract process, and the tendency for disputes.
- The third one is reshaping the trust behaviour from human trust to a computer coding trust, especially with the self-executing mechanism. Thus, instead of relying on human trust between parties, which may also include an intermediary such as lawyers, parties to a contract rely on the self-execution of the smart contract based on the computer codes and instructions incorporated.

Conclusion

The smart contract which was built in blockchain technology is mostly associated with cryptocurrencies 'since it was created as an enabler for them'. Cryptocurrencies are, however, just one of several applications of the technology. The technology is, in its fundamental state, a shared, distributed ledger, that is peer-to-peer replicated against each other. Blockchain is built upon a consensus model, which means that all nodes need to agree on the true version of the ledger, which eliminates the trust-based model that most transactions rely on today. Different types of blockchains provide different types of features and benefits. Features such as smart contracts, supply chain transparency and record-keeping are very valuable for different industrial contexts. This chapter reviewed how smart contracts can prevent or mitigate issues related to sustainability within the construction industry. Also, the challenges in the implementation of smart contract were vividly explored in the course of this chapter presentation.

References

Cardeira, H. (2015). *Smart contracts and their applications in the construction industry.* Retrieved from http://www.google.com/smart-contract-and-their-applications

Dhillon, V., Metcalf, D., & Hooper, M. (2017). Blockchain enabled applications. In *Understand the blockchain ecosystem and how to make it work for you.* New York, NY: Apress.

Domashova, D. V., Pisarchik, E. E., & Lifar, A. V. (2018). Technology for automated search and detection of overpriced road construction and repair public procurement contracts. *Journal of Social Sciences, 3*(2), 458–466.

Gupta, M. (2017). *Blockchain for dummies.* Retrieved from https://www-01.ibm.com/common/ssi/cgi-bin/ssialias?htmlfid=XIM12354USEN

Lamb, K. (2018). *Blockchain and smart contracts: What the AEC sector needs to know.* Retrieved from http://respository.cam.ac.uk

Laurence, T. (2017). *Blockchain.* Hoboken, NJ: John Wiley and Sons.

Liu, H., & Zhao, C. Q. (2014). The application of information management in construction contracts management. *Applied Mechanics and Materials, 584*(16), 2490–2493.

Mason, J., & Escott, H. (2018). *Smart contracts in construction: A single source of truth or mere double speak?* Retrieved from https://pig-uat.opencloudcrm.co.uk

Mik, E. (2017). Smart contracts: Terminology, technical limitations and real world complexity. *Law, Innovation and Technology, 9*(2), 269–300.

Morabito, V. (2017). *Business innovation through blockchain: The B³ perspective.* Cham: Springer International Publishing.

Oke, A. E., Aigbavboa, C. O., Stephen, S. S., & Thwala, W. D. (2021). *Sustainable construction in the era of the fourth industrial revolution.* London, New York, NY: Taylor and Francis Group. doi:10.1201/9781003179849-1

Presley, A., & Meade, L. (2010). Benchmarking for sustainability: An application to the sustainable construction industry. *An International Journal of Benchmarking, 7*(3), 435–451.

Ryan, P. (2017). Smart contract relations in e-commerce: Legal implications of exchanges conducted on the blockchain. *Technology Innovation Management Review, 7*(10), 14–21.

Sears, S. K., Sears, G. A., Clough, R. H., Rounds, J. L., & Segner, R. O. (2015). *Construction project management* (6th ed.). New York, NY: John Wiley and Sons.

Sklaroff, J. M. (2017). *Smart contracts and the cost of inflexibility.* Retrieved from https://scholarship.law.upenn.edu/prize_papers/9

Sun, M., & Oza, T. (2010). User survey: The benefits of an online collaborative contract change management system. *Journal of Information Technology in Construction (ITcon), 15*(19), 258–268.

Szabo, N. (1997). *Formalizing and securing relationships on public networks.* Retrieved from http://firstmonday.org

Vogelsang, M. (2010). *Digitalization in open economies: Theory and policy implications* (1st ed.). New York, NY: Physica-Verlag.

Wang, J., Wu, P., Wang, X., & Shou, W. (2017). The outlook of blockchain technology for construction engineering management. *Frontiers of Engineering Management, 4*(1), 67–75.

Yih Chong, H., Balamuralithara, B., & Choy Chong, S. (2011). Construction contract administration in Malaysia using DFD: A conceptual model. *Industrial Management and Data Systems, 111*(9), 1449–1464.

Chapter 9

Quantum Computing for Sustainable Infrastructure Management

Abstract

Quantum computer design is a registration that utilises quantum-mechanical wonder, like superposition and entrapment, used to arrange the assets of a quantum computer. A deliberate layered system can be planned to handle the difficulties, which emerge during the advancement of a quantum figuring. The plan usefulness is isolated into layers where the subsystems are planned in such a manner with the goal that it can investigate the issues freely and measures better between the layers bringing about a superior arrangement. Right now, all adaptable quantum figuring innovations are recommendations and critical advances in assembling necessities needed to carry them to the real world. By and by, a few recommendations have less cumbersome innovative obstacles before them than others. Even though its applications are somewhat limited in the construction industry, steps have been taken towards its implementation across the industry as well as other industries.

Keywords: Construction computing; construction engineering; quantum computing; quantum error correction; quantum computer architecture; sustainable construction

Introduction

Quantum processing is considered the space of study which centres on creating computer innovations that are dependent on standards related to the quantum hypothesis. In this type of processing, the energy and subsequent matter on the number and size of the quantum present in nuclear and subatomic levels are presented clearly. In the old-style computer model, the most essential structure block is known as the bit. It has just two particular states, for example a 0 or a 1. In a quantum computer, the standards do not continue as before. In quantum registering, a quantum bit is alluded to as a Qubit. It can just exist in the traditional 0 and 1 states. It can likewise be in a reasonable superposition of both

A Digital Path to Sustainable Infrastructure Management, 85–92
Copyright © 2024 Ayodeji E. Oke and Seyi S. Stephen
Published under exclusive licence by Emerald Publishing Limited
doi:10.1108/978-1-83797-703-120241009

(Cohen, Khan, & Alexander, 2019). The quantum data contain certain calculations and activities, which are not feasible for old-style data. Of the recognized quantum calculations, two of them stand apart to be the most helpful considering huge numbers and re-enactment of quantum science. The first is valuable because of its ability to mask cryptographic codes, while then again the subsequent one can help in empowering of reproducing extraordinary compounds and organic sciences like the plan of sub-atomic level medications and nanostructured materials. Along these lines, this chapter examines the structure through which the difficulties of planning a quantum computer can be tended to. The possibility of engineering is one, which decays the conduct of a mind-boggling framework into a bunch of tasks (Steane, 2007). The reason for a layered design is to acquire similar utilising a bunch of layers where each layer will comprise a specific capacity.

History Evolution of Quantum Computer Architecture

The enormous measure of handling power, which is created by computer-producing organisations, has not yet had the option to fulfil the prerequisite of boundaries like speed and processing. In 1947, American computer engineer Howard Aiken referenced that only six electronic computerised computers would have the option to fulfil the registering needs of the United States (Zaborniak & De Sousa, 2021). Moore's Law expresses that the quantity of semiconductors on a chip keeps on multiplying like clockwork. This outcome in the year 2020 or 2030 will discover the circuits on a chip estimated on a nuclear scale.

Since Vincenzo's presentation of major measures for quantum processing innovation, Yang et al. (2021) and Steane (2007) delineated that it is so hard to plan a framework that is fit for running a quantum mistake rectification enough (Sama, 2021a, 2021b); other gatherings of specialists have laid out different scientific categorisations for the need of enormous scope frameworks (Sama, 2020a, 2020b). A portion of the specialists additionally chipped away at the fact that it is so hard to move the information in a quantum processor.

New Trends in Construction

Digitalisation offers significant upgrades in construction through its numerous benefits achieved set within standards and efficiency (Oke, Aigbavboa, Stephen, & Thwala, 2021). Following a tempestuous year of changing estimates and evolving assumptions, the year 2021 will be an extended time of reappearance and development in the construction business due to the outbreak of COVID-19. This pandemic changed the outlook of the construction process from the usual to a more technologically advanced platform.

In coping with the aftermath of this threat, many construction firms and other industries developed several strategic policies within the system of practice or management practices usually embraced in managing disasters just like the pandemic mentioned. This gave rise to construction expenses and work deficiencies persevere, provoking the business to enhance cutthroat groundbreaking thoughts, while stricter guidelines add to a diminished edge for blunder and waste. Strategic flexibility, value management and embracing technological trends are some of the practices engaged in by professionals in the construction industry. With this, the prevalence of these technological practices changes the construction site, contract administration and execution, workforce management and net revenues amongst many other effects experienced in technologically engaged practices. Some of these trends commonly used are expatiated below (Oke et al., 2021):

Smart Contracts

As earlier described in the previous chapter of this book, specialists see block-chain technology as a catalyst that is developing connections in the construction business – it is an amazing part in giving a safer and quick work process that permits all elaborate gatherings admittance to further developed efficiency. The introduction of smart contracts in construction will enhance swift contract-related execution in construction with little or no mistakes. Also, smart contracts open the construction professionals to better contractual arrangements and agreements within a centralised framework fused into working concerning set purchase, tract and payment. Through a distributed contractual execution, the smart contract blockchain works in providing closure, better undertaking, expanded security, swift payment, faster closeouts and robotised store network controlled within a sizeable number of participants.

Construction Drones

Drones are used in construction to monitor, take aerial views, inspect set-out activities and record on construction sites. Through automated systems, drones (either manned or unmanned) are designed to carry out specific instructions encoded in programming over a targeted area. Information collected when the drone is deployed on a construction site can aid in the decision-making mechanism and further propel whole construction measures and practices concerning achieving a desirable project at completion.

Individual security and ineffective supervision pose the greatest liabilities during construction. Drones can perform occupations instead of human specialists to foresee possible injury or faults on construction sites. For example, in a bid to save cost, a contractor decided against maintaining standards on a concrete raft by using a mixing ratio of 1:4:8 rather than the 1:2:4 specified in the contract. While both the skilled and unskilled laborers were about to start casting, the professionals in control of the drone discovered this and decided to take immediate action by stopping the construction process. This swift action has saved the raft from future collapse which might result in extra cost or even loss of lives.

Augmented Reality (AR)

AR is the presentation of abstract concepts in reality within a systemised or computerised platform. The AR provides a sense of better interaction between the design team and the other parties involved in the project (contractor, client, value manager, project managers, builders, etc.). Here, the intended project is projected at a clear angle (mostly 360-degree) for better assessment by the construction team. This aids in decision-making on the type of design, materials, nature and functionalities, feasibility and viability of a design in terms of cost, quality and duration.

For manufacturers and designers, AR works with the utilisation of wearable technology and 360-degree video to empower:

- 3D representation of future tasks on their general climate,
- Computerised estimating of structures,
- Quick and moderate recreation of compositional and primary changes,
- Security preparing and danger reproductions, and
- Building Information Modelling (BIM).

Remote Worksites and Mobile Access

Portable applications in the construction business permit worksite access more than ever conceivable, including continuous examinations, on-location responsibility and exact estimations taken from a cell phone camera. AECOM created technology that considers public endorsement gatherings to occur so open undertakings can keep on pushing ahead without in-person social occasions. Other versatile applications in the commercial centre incorporate estimating aid AirMeasure and resource the board programming Infotycoon. Those without a complete versatile network will be at an efficiency and deal detriment going ahead.

Rising Material Costs

Material prices have been fluctuating over the years due to many factors. Inflation, demand and supply, aesthetics, fiscal policies and project area are some of the common factors that gave rise to material costs in both developed and developing nature of the world. Also, as the construction industry tends towards sustainable construction, and with the demand for these sustainable materials, the prices of these materials are greatly affected in the market. With the prices affected, construction processes are also on the rise, and this sometimes forces the construction professionals involved in a project to obtain loans from different institutions to meet the set project duration and quality. However, loan fees are probably going to accumulate a wide range of expenses, bringing about additional tension on complete construction. Advances like robots, AR and BIM will demonstrate the key to assisting with keeping up with project volume and battling this expense pressure.

Concentrating majorly on inventive materials and technologies might push up costs further despite the fact that they at last give more reserve funds to clients over the long haul. A portion of these inventive materials include:

- Self-mending concrete,
- 3D printing,
- Straightforward aluminum,
- Light creating concrete, and
- Imperceptible sunlight based cells.

Smart Cities

Great technological organisations on the planet such as IBM, Microsoft, Cisco, etc. are putting vigorous efforts into megaprojects to assemble keen, reasonable urban areas. These urban areas are more many-sided and interconnected than most megaprojects and also require extreme arranging and advancement preceding the beginning. Oke, Stephen, Aigbavboa, Ogunsemi, and Aje (2022) described the concept of a smart city as that which encompasses the integration of automated frameworks with human interactions to create cities that are not only functional towards survival but also that which is sustainable even for the generations unborn.

Construction industry patterns are quickly changing the worldwide market; rising costs and gifted work deficiencies are probably going to proceed in the coming decade, and administrative difficulties might become stricter with an exceptional investigation on work environment security and environmental change variation. By taking on new works on utilising innovations and putting resources into new undertakings, manufacturers and designers can decrease hazards, win more agreements and appreciate benefits, especially when a concept like that of a smart city is fully in motion.

Details of Quantum Computing

Detailing the expected operations and systems in quantum computing, the criteria embedded are summarised below:

- Quantum computing must be a real system that is versatile with clear qubits,
- Before its computation, its state must be realisable,
- There must be sufficient de-coherence time,
- Have a far reaching game plan of quantum entryways,
- Permits assessment in high capability,
- Presence of alternatives and changes within recognized qubits (fixed and moving), and
- Transfer of genuine affirmation of qubits between identified regions (Cohen et al., 2019; Steane, 2007).

Quantum Computing in Today's World

Computerised figuring has limits regarding a huge order of assessment called combinatorics, in which the solicitation for data is basic to the best course of action. This, however, gives rise to calculations that can take even the fastest computers a long time to gauge. Quantum advancement is pushing towards the norm of efficiency across platforms.

Quantum Computing and Drivers in Construction

It is broadly accepted that quantum computers, and quantum gadgets as a general rule, can beat their traditional partners. Some issues can be settled productively by quantum computers. Old-style computers require a sizeable information to process an output, while this is not the same in quantum computers. In construction especially, combinatorics in quantum computing will aid faster and less expensive assessment of construction contracts, designs algorithms, project evaluations and decision-making in terms of calculations about the strength of the materials as well as the building in general (Moore, 2019). However, this type of computing is generally not popular amongst construction professionals concerning participants in developing countries. Cost of acquisition and setting, skilled personnel, adherence, etc. are some of the barriers to its implementation in the construction industry. As much as barriers are easily identified due to similarities with other technology adoption in most construction industries, the drivers to this computing will be listed below but not limited to:

- Interchangeability between artificial intelligence (AI) and quantum computers,
- Quantum cryptography for security,
- Subsidising for quantum innovative work,
- Finding new atoms by reenactment, and
- Advancing the prescriptions for restoring the sicknesses.

Scientists need to assess the cooperation between atoms, proteins and synthetic compounds to check whether medications will work on specific conditions or fix sicknesses to foster a viable medication. To dissect the exceptional measure of mixes of particles for prescriptions, it requires some investment and work seriously. Since quantum computers can at the same time look at numerous particles, proteins and synthetic compounds which assist physicists with recognising reasonable medication alternatives quicker, the computational done by quantum computers would permit the qualities of an individual to be sequenced and broken down a lot quicker than the strategies that we are utilising today and would permit the improvement of customised drugs.

Applications in Construction

Existing 'old style' figuring, while amazingly mind-blowing, has certain typical cutoff focuses. There are necessities to how speedy computations can be performed, or the level of complexity to the mathematical issues they try to handle. Quantum enlisting takes advantage of parts of quantum real effects, to make processors that go past zeros and ones, on a very basic level extending the power, speed and refinement of the calculations they can do. As quantum computers are growing rapidly from 'interesting speculation' to 'genuine development', it is a pleasant opportunity to look at how they might change longstanding issues looked at by trained professionals and organisers across the manufactured environment. It can further be applied in areas as benefits in Moore (2019):

- It helps in swift calculations and evaluations of project estimations,
- It helps in the detection of corrosion,
- More efficient surveying,
- Better planning and organisation,
- Faster completion times, and
- Bringing of early stages prospects beneficial in the construction process.

Challenges of Quantum Computing

- Possible interaction with environment and thus lose coherence,
- Skilled personnel to handle operations,
- Difficulty in copying stored and manipulated information,
- Difficulty in maintaining entangled and super-positioned states persistently, and
- Requires massive cooling due to its bulky nature.

Conclusion

Quantum computing is still in the lab of scientists, researchers and engineers on how to optimise the use of the growing technology and apply it in the construction sector. However, early signs have shown that it can facilitate quick planning and execution of numerous activities related to construction in terms of surveying, design communication, data storage, estimations, etc. as well as other industries like pharmaceutical, engineering, data science and so on. Even as studies are still very much needed to maximise its applications across these industries, construction professionals can be sensitised about the potential influence it will have on project executions within coordinated systems centred towards swift and sustainable project implementation.

References

Cohen, J., Khan, A., & Alexander, C. (2019). *Uncovering the value of quantum technologies.* Retrieved from https://chicagoquantum.medium.com/uncovering-the-business-value-of-quantum-technologies-9646638f0abc

Moore, S. (2019). *Utilizing quantum computing in the construction industry.* Retrieved from https://www.disruptionhub.com/quantum-technologies-change-your-industry-rhys-lewis/

Oke, A. E., Aigbavboa, C. O., Stephen, S. S., & Thwala, W. D. (2021). *Sustainable construction in the era of the fourth industrial revolution.* London, New York: Taylor and Francis Group. doi:10.1201/9781003179849-1

Oke, A. E., Stephen, S. S., Aigbavboa, C. O., Ogunsemi, D. R., & Aje, I. O. (2022). *Smart cities: A panacea for sustainable construction.* Bingley: Emerald Publishing Limited.

Sama, A. (2020a). *Meneropong Masa Depan: Quantum computing.* Retrieved from https://andisama.medium.com

Sama, A. (2020b). *Hello tomorrow, I am a hybrid quantum machine learning.* Retrieved from https://andisama.medium.com

Sama, A. (2021a). *Star trek and the no-cloning theorem.* Retrieved from https://andisama.com

Sama, A. (2021b). *Quantum computing: Communication and sensing.* Retrieved from https://andisama.medium.com

Steane, A. M. (2007). How to build a 300 bit, 1 giga-operation quantum computer. *Quantum Information and Computation, 7*(2), 171–185.

Yang, Y., Shen, Z., Zhu, X., Deng, C., Liu, S., & An, Q. (2021). An FPGA-based low latency AWG for superconducting quantum computers. In *2021 Institute of Electrical and Electronics Engineers IEEE International Instrumentation and Measurement Technology Conference (I2MTC)*, China (pp. 1–6). doi:10.1109/I2MTC50364.2021.9460084

Zaborniak, T., & De Sousa, R. (2021). Benchmarking Hamiltonian noise in the D-Wave quantum annealer. *Institute of Electrical and Electronics Engineers IEEE Transactions on Quantum Engineering, 2*(1), 1–6.

Chapter 10

Smart Computing for Sustainable Infrastructure Management

Abstract

The construction industry has a fragmented nature which accounts for the highest degree of decentralisation of information. The exchange of information can be made possible and easier by the application of smart computing into the construction process. This creates an opportunity to enhance productivity and communication among stakeholders of the industry. This chapter, therefore, explores the concept of smart contracts, its drivers, challenges and critical success factors for implementing smart computing into construction in the effort to work towards an industry that is functional and sustainable at the same time.

Keywords: Construction transformation; digital construction; industrial revolution; information technology; smart computation; sustainable construction

Introduction

The construction industry has the highest degree of decentralisation of information when compared to some other industries such as manufacturing, financial, media and entertainment and software (Box, 2014). This indicates that information is distributed within means in construction organisations. Furthermore, Box (2014) mentioned another important variable in terms of mobility. The researcher expatiated that the construction industry has the highest rate of mobile content access, as the stakeholders interact and access contents related to project planning, execution and management by the use of mobile devices more than any other sectors of the economy. With the use of computers and related technologies, the construction industry and human life are changing rapidly, becoming faster and smarter than ever before.

Computers transformed the entire world into a global village. Audio-visual communication between persons in any part of the world in almost no time has

A Digital Path to Sustainable Infrastructure Management, 93–103

Copyright © 2024 Ayodeji E. Oke and Seyi S. Stephen

Published under exclusive licence by Emerald Publishing Limited

doi:10.1108/978-1-83797-703-120241010

become possible due to computers. Computers are being used in the area of art and culture, finance, print, electronic and digital media, entertainment, medical and healthcare, education, transport, law and order, defence, research, innovations and many more to mention. Construction projects and human life gained momentum and became easier, simpler and smarter as a result of the application of computing-related practices to events. As any technology is a double-edged sword, there are a few threats like security, data loss, system failures, etc. that needs to be addressed when discussing technology and its consequences. These challenges have limited the full adoption of computing systems into some construction industries as many construction professionals still struggle with coming to terms with its benefits outweighing its problems.

Mainframe computing, personal computing and network computing are the earlier computing programmes used. However, smart computing technology is the most recent and rapidly developing innovation and growth technology addressing the previously unresolved issues. Computing today incorporates the use of various techniques such as:

- Machine learning,
- Soft computing,
- Artificial intelligence (AI),
- Pattern recognition,
- Robotics,
- Machine vision,
- Simulation and modelling,
- Biomedical computing,
- Signal and image processing,
- Bioinformatics,
- Green computing,
- Ubiquitous computing,
- Cryptography, and other techniques.

Also, hybridised techniques have been added into computing through:

- Swarm optimisation,
- Ant colony,
- Evolutionary algorithm, and
- Nature inspired computing solving the real-life problems with the help of intelligence and smart science.

Smart computing utilises the power of microelectronics in coordination with many advanced and hybrid computing techniques (Chatterjee & Nath, 2014). Present in this chapter is how smart computing works, smart computing in construction, drivers of smart computing application in construction and benefits and challenges of encounter in its application.

How Smart Computing Works

'Smart computing technology' is related to computer hardware and software; also, it can sometimes be both. It is the perfect blend of existing technologies with newer concepts for achieving enhanced computing operations. Self-monitoring, analysing and reporting technologies (SMARTs) are also known as smart computing technology (SCT). Fig. 1 shows what SMARTs do as it monitors and detects reliability, anticipate failures of computer hard disk drives (HDDs), solid-state drives (SSDs), and embedded multimedia cards (eMMC) drives and reports accordingly to the user. Its main function is to detect and report various indicators that drive reliability with the purpose of anticipating potential hardware failures. On indication of upcoming failures of the drive, software running on the host system notifies the user well in advance and alerts the user to take

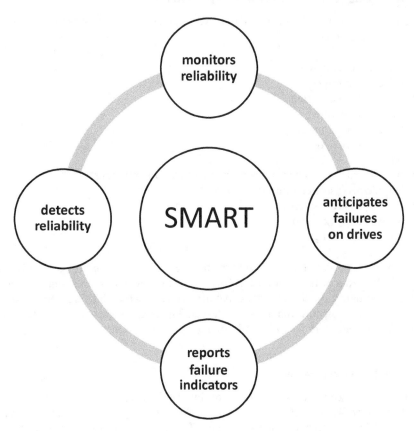

Fig. 1.   Showing What Self-monitoring, Analysing and Reporting
Technologies (SMARTs) Do.

precautionary action against data loss. With this information, the failing drive can be replaced and data veracity maintained (Nikki, 2014).

Smart computing is a new generation technology of integrated hardware, software and network technologies that provide information technology systems with real-time awareness of the real world and advanced analytics to help people make more intelligent decisions about alternatives and actions resulting in the optimisation of processes. With smart computing, existing technologies gain new capabilities of real-time situational awareness and automated analysis. In smart computing, instead of giving task solutions to be performed, it goes one step ahead and initiates the best possible action. It senses the happenings around, gathers the new information, analyses it further for risks and possibilities, suggests alternatives and finely takes an appropriate action (Nikki, 2014).

Supporting Programmes and Applications

SCT is a multidisciplinary domain. It works in combination of latest in sensor based technologies in:

- Internet of Things,
- Edge computing,
- Cyber-Physical system,
- Machine Learning,
- Cognitive Computing,
- Big Data analytics,
- AI,
- Algorithmic and system advancements of cloud computing,
- Mobile/pervasive computing,
- Cyber-physical systems,
- Sensor networks, and
- Social computing.

These systems are taking technology to a new dimension for improved ways of living. In terms of the relationship between smart computing and some technologies, the narrations below give expatiated benefits when they are combined to function as a unit towards a goal or target. The technologies identified here are artificial recognition, face recognition and cloud computing.

Smart Computing and AI

Using high-speed hardware does not by itself guarantee a solution to the particular problem quickly nor does it simplify the programming process. In this view, AI-based software systems could be of much help and perform on their own and complete a few tasks such as bookkeeping, configuration control and internal structuring tasks swiftly with or without assistance. Without AI-powered systems, these tasks are usually carried out by programmers (Robert & Kahn, 1983).

Smart Computing and Face Recognition

Using face recognition systems instead of just for identification and surveillance tasks can function further in interpreting human actions, intentions and behaviour at the core of SCTs. Facial expression recognition system interacts with smart environment capabilities. For example, a smart system knows whether the user is impatient as the information is delivered slowly or swiftly, or whether the user is confused because it is coming at a particular speed. Facial expressions provide clues for identifying and distinguishing between these states. The best facial expression recognition and analysing system must first be able to recognise and tune its parameters to a specific person and this is what is offered in the application of smart computing into the face recognition system. Face recognition is an integral part of wearable systems like memory aids and context-aware systems. Such smart computing systems are useful for patients suffering from Alzheimer's disease (Nikki, 2014).

Cloud-Based Smart Mobile Computing

Mobile Cloud Computing (MCC) integrates cloud computing technology and ubiquitous mobile networks into overcoming environment certain issues related to performance, security and of course certain limitations to battery life, storage capacity, bandwidth, etc. with cloud computing data processing and storage happening outside the device. Google's Gmail, maps and navigation systems for mobile, voice search, android platform applications such as Mobile from Apple, Live Mesh from Microsoft, Motoblur from Motorola, mobile accounting, mobile payment and mobile healthcare such as monitoring of patients activity, playing music, shopping, advertising, ticketing, gaming, learning and voice-based searching based on speech recognition are served to users and are powered by MCC (Nikki, 2014).

Applications of Smart Computing in Construction Using Business Intelligence (BI)

BI is all about delivering the right information, i.e. relevant, required and reliable information to the right people at the right time to achieve smarter and better decisions. To achieve this, BI makes use of a set of concepts, procedures and methods to improve business decision-making by using fact-based support systems. In other words, it uses methods and programmes to collect unstructured data, convert it into information and present it to improve business decisions (Chatterjee & Nath, 2014). BI can be described as the processes, technologies and tools required to turn data into information and then subsequently turn the information into knowledge and the latter into plans that drive profitable business actions (Chatterjee & Nath, 2014).

In this century, computational capabilities and digital technologies are used extensively for technical, industrial and construction development. This century has shown a typical characteristic of a rapid shift from the traditional construction industrial model brought about by the industrial revolution through industrialisation and information-based technology. The onset of the information age or digital age is marked by rapid digitisation due to the digital revolution. The evolutions and advancements in computational and digital technologies have an extensive impact on the day-to-day life of construction activities. This, in turn, has led to the fact that modernisation and advancements in information and communication processes have become the driving force for societal evolution, progress, growth and development. Today construction industry has shifted its business strategies from traditional bricks and mortar to digital and online business or more specifically e-commerce. Online transactions i.e. buying and selling of construction materials and products over the internet, electronic funds transfer, online banking (net banking and mobile banking) and modern business activities such as online marketing, transaction processing, material management, supply chain management, inventory management, production and logistics management, as well as automated data collection systems are used extensively thereby generating an enormous amount of data (Chatterjee & Nath, 2014).

Earlier construction employees had to go through complex webs of linked spreadsheets, a huge bulk of documents, to prepare organisational reports after analysing the data manually. But with the advent of BI systems, employees can now request any required information and they will get it in no time. BI offers a significant advantage by:

- Helping to make strategic decisions,
- Providing real-time access to organised data,
- Automated preparation of reports and charts for construction firms' dashboards,
- Tracking key performance indicators (KPIs),
- Continuous performance monitoring,
- Management and lots more.

Besides these benefits, using BI, the user can discover inefficient firm processes, and construction issues, identify areas of strength and weaknesses, and discover new opportunities which will contribute to a better understanding of the construction firm's operations and market challenges. Today, construction firms primarily focus on the construction-value perspective, and hence they use BI to enhance their decision-making capabilities for managerial processes such as planning, purchasing, budgeting, assessing, controlling, measuring and monitoring activities. With the use of digital technologies, construction firms today are generating numerous data sufficient for the project (Chatterjee & Nath, 2014).

The primary benefits of using BI are be as follow:

- Enhance decision-making mechanism,
- Enhance operational efficiency by optimising internal business processes,
- Improve revenue generation as it incorporates new business strategies,

- Improve business competitive advantages in the market against rivals,
- Identifies with current market trends through customers and behavioural analyses, and
- Procures solutions to identified business problems.

Benefits of Smart Computing for Construction Project

Smart computing can be essential across industries in maintain and improving operations, the construction industry can also benefit from its application in terms of cost, mobility, flexibility and maintenance and updating as illustrated by Cheng and Kumar (2012).

Cost Reduction

The conventional way of information technology (IT) delivery presents a major difference from the smart computing model mainly because of the utility-based pricing model of such a model. Most architectural engineering and construction (AEC) companies are small medium enterprises (SMEs) with relative employees and budgets; hence these features are crucial barriers to the adoption of IT in the AEC industry. Smart computing presents itself as a solution that addresses this vital issue for the construction industry (Cheng & Kumar, 2012). Currently, smart computer users pay the service providers based on a monthly or annual subscription, with the payment dependent on the number of IT resources and time that are used. Traditionally, companies make payments at the time when they purchase software and hardware systems. The initial investment is redeemed eventually depending on the designated usage duration of the systems. Enabling smart computer users to pay monthly or for their usage, allow them to switch to cheaper options whenever available or required. The user can also terminate the contract earlier if the service providers finish the project within a shorter timeframe (Cheng & Kumar, 2012).

System Mobility

In a smart computing environment, systems and programmes operate on the clouds and other software. This means that end users can access the same information from different locations and run computationally demanding applications such as structural analysis only by using a web-enabled device, e.g. desktop computers or smart phones.

System Flexibility

The level of IT that a project needs varies throughout its lifecycle, hence the convenience of smart computing-based resources. These resources can be flexibly deployed and terminated, as well as scaled up and down. Consequently, IT cost changes to a variable cost rather than a fixed cost.

System Maintenance

Infrastructure as a service (IAAS) and platform as a service (PAAS) providers continuously maintain their systems and deliver IT resources such as central processing units (CPUs), memory and operating systems as individual services. As a result, this avoids the 'disposal of companies' obsolete computers and continuous installation of patches for operating systems'.

Challenges of Smart Computing

Smart computing presents significant risks and challenges. According to a survey of nearly 1800 US businesses and IT professionals by the Information Systems Audit and Control Association (Information Systems Audit and Control Association ISACA, 2010), 45% of the respondents identified the risks involved in the use of smart computing in any industry whatsoever. In addition, Brender and Markov (2013) established the main topics of concern regarding the adoption of smart computing from a management point of view regarding information security, privileged user access, regulatory compliance, data location, investigative support, availability and disaster recovery and providers' lock-in and long-term viability.

Information Security

Information security is one of the major concerns regarding the adoption of smart computing. The technology's presence on the internet and the substantial concentration of data present an attractive target for hackers (European Network and Information SecurityAgency (ENISA), 2009). According to Caroll, Der Merwe, and Kotze (2011), information security is rated as a top threat in interviews with South African participants. In addition, Sultan (2010) cited a survey carried out by the international data corporation (IDC) where around 75% of respondents said they had concerns about security in the application of smart computing for their operations.

Privileged User Access

Another identified risk is privileged user access. This denotes the existing risk of a malicious insider (personnel) who may cause brand damage, and financial and productivity losses to a SC customer (Hubbard & Sutton, 2010). For a better understanding, it is necessary to remember that the processing of sensitive data outside the premises of a company bypasses the security controls that an in-house IT department employs. Hence a good practice for customers is to procure information on the hiring and oversight of privileged cloud administrators (Bhadra & Mohammed, 2020). A solution established for this concern is the use of the least privilege principle, which proposes granting to individuals or processes the minimum privileges and resources for the minimum period required to complete a task (Marinescu, 2018).

Regulatory Compliance

Regulatory audit compliance is an important concern among cloud sub-contractors. According to Heiser and Nicolett (2008), traditional software providers such as cloud providers have to submit to security certifications and external audits and provide customers with information about the security controls that have been evaluated. Regarding privacy regulations in different jurisdictions, data location is a big concern among companies subcontracting such software services. One example is the data held in US-based data centres, which may be accessed by the US government as provided by the Patriot Act.

Data Location

EU governments have privacy regulations that prohibit the release of certain data outside of the EU. Consequently, companies like Amazon and Microsoft allow their customers to choose the 'physical location of the data (e.g. the European Union or United States)'.

Availability and Disaster Recovery

The availability of SCT services is an important point of concern for businesses, especially for critical business processes. Bhadra and Mohammed (2020) suggested that any enterprise procuring outsourcing critical business processes to the computing technology software should establish together with the provider a service level agreement (SLA) for the availability of service critical for business processes. In addition, a further study by Hubbard and Sutton (2010) considered availability and disaster recovery as critical areas after being ranked second after information security by 66.7% of the respondents. Also, Prakash (2011) established the importance for a business to require information on 'what happens to their data in case of disaster and how long' the recovery process could last. This would help them to know what information is to be inputted and vice versa which thus affects business performance.

Additional Risks and Challenges

After analysing a study conducted by the consulting firm, Cambridge Technology Partners about Swiss businesses' engagement in SC, Brender and Markov (2013) observed several legal, technical and operational risks or threats in migrating to a cloud service. The original study submitted five reports analysing the risks and challenges, and proposed mitigation practices in the adoption of SC services by five companies based in Switzerland. Two of these companies were considered SMEs and the other three as economically significant enterprises. The risks summarised by Brender and Markov (2013) are:

- Teething problems,
- Application performance of the SC,

- Loss of governance,
- Determination of the competent authorities in case of conflict,
- Cost,
- Economic denial of service,
- Data segregation,
- Data destruction,
- Data traceability,
- Security during data transportation,
- Security of financial transactions,
- Physical security, and
- Natural disasters.

Conclusion

SCT is a new generational computing technology that integrates existing computer-related hardware and software technologies into various computer architectures, networking systems and modules. Smart computing performs data processing faster and in a smarter way giving real-time and the best possible solutions with safety, security and cost-effectively. It is the computing technology of the future integrated slowly into construction and other industries for expected benefits and significance.

References

Bhadra, S., & Mohammed, S. (2020). Cloud computing threats and risks: Uncertainty and uncontrollability in the risk society. *Electronics Journal, 7*(2), 1047–1071.

Box, I. (2014). *The information economy: A study of five industries.* Retrieved from https://www.box.com/blog/mapping-the-information-economy-a-tale-of-five-industries

Brender, N., & Markov, I. (2013). Risk perception and risk management in cloud computing: Results from a case study of Swiss companies. *International Journal of Information Management, 33*(5), 726–733.

Caroll, M., Der Merwe, A. V., & Kotze, P. (2011). *Secure cloud computing: Benefits, risks and controls.* Retrieved from https://www.ieeexlore.ieee.org

Chatterjee, P., & Nath, A. (2014). Application of smart computing in Indian railway system. *Computer Science and Economics, 1*(5), 148–155.

Cheng, J. C., & Kumar, B. (2012). Mobile and pervasive computing in construction. *Cloud Computing Support for Construction Collaboration, 1*(1), 237–254. doi:10.1002/9781118422281.Ch12

European Network and Information Security Agency (ENISA). (2009). *Cloud computing: Benefits, risks and recommendations for information security.* Retrieved from https://www.enisa.europa.eu

Heiser, J., & Nicollett, M. (2008). *Assessing the security risks of cloud computing.* Retrieved from http://cloud.ctrls.in/files/assessing-the-security-risks.pdf

Hubbard, D., & Sutton, M. (2010). *Top threats to smart computing: Cloud security alliance*. Retrieved from https://cloudsecurityalliance.org/topthreats/csathreats. v1.0.pdf

Information Systems Audit and Control Association ISACA. (2010). *The information systems audit and control association United States IT risk/reward barometer survey*. Retrieved from https://www.isaca.org

Marinescu, D. C. (2018). Cloud security. *Cloud Computing Theory and Practice, 5*(1), 405–437. doi:10.1016/B978-0-12-812810-7.00015-7

Nikki, L. (2014). *Mobile cloud computing applications for smart computing*. Retrieved from https://www.thescholedge.org

Prakash, S. (2011). *Risk management: Cloud computing considerations*. Retrieved from https://www.infoworld.com

Robert, E., & Kahn, L. (1983). New generation in computer. *Institute of Electrical and Electronics Engineers (IEEE) Spectrum, 20*(11), 36–41.

Sultan, N. (2010). Cloud computing for education: A new dawn? *International Journal of Information Management, 30*(2), 109–116.

Chapter 11

Cognitive Radio for Sustainable Infrastructure Management

Abstract

This chapter presented cognitive radio networks in construction. The construction industry requires an efficient bandwidth of wireless technology for effectiveness without delay. The persistence of challenges with the investment in third generation is a great concern, and this chapter identified investing in fifth generation (as an alternative) to enlarge bandwidth for better effectiveness that is capable of dealing with unavailable or scarcity of radio spectrum. The application of fifth generation will permit efficient utilisation of the radio spectrum by the primary and secondary users to detect the spectrum parameters which will highlight the direct and adequate interaction with the radio channel. This chapter further considered the usage of this technology as it relates to permitting sharing of sense in the spectrum.

Keywords: Cognitive radio; application; cognitive radio network; cognitive radio in construction; spectrum sensing techniques; cognitive radio challenges and benefits

Introduction

Cognitive radio is a technological development that focuses on fighting for a space in the radio spectrum with the aid of dynamic spectrum access (Han & Liu, 2008). Wireless local area network (WLAN) has brought attractiveness to cognitive radio due to their usage of unoccupied and available channels in a wide range of 10 megahertz to about 10 gigahertz frequency. This was achieved through the detection of available channels before launching into communication proper (Haykin, 2005). Specifically, cognitive radio is a technological sensor that has enormous strength to enhance communication. It has also comprehended the effective usage of the spectrum to the fullest without interfering with the primary users simply because of its capacity to disruptive of transmitted parameters within the environment. It was reported according to Granelli (2010) that the high level

A Digital Path to Sustainable Infrastructure Management, 105–109
Copyright © 2024 Ayodeji E. Oke and Seyi S. Stephen
Published under exclusive licence by Emerald Publishing Limited
doi:10.1108/978-1-83797-703-120241011

of complexities in construction projects necessitated cognitive radio which added more technology improvement in project implementation.

Due to the unrelenting growth of technologies within the spectrum, allocating specific services to the available frequency without interfering with the primary users showed that the authorised spectrum is yet to be fully used in the geographical dimension. Improvement arises through the utilisation of spectrum, peradventure if the secondary users could make use of the licenced band of the primary users when not available due to the proposed promotion of cognitive radio having enough technology in spectrum utilisation coupled with cognitive radio adaptively to the environment, it is capable in occupying any available space within the spectrum without creating a hazard to the licenced operators in the spectrum (Mitola & Maguire, 1999).

Cognitive Radio in Construction

In the study by Shepard (2014), in construction, the interrelations of available signals within its local environment arise due to the method applied for the cognitive radio. The use of the Kriging method came often due to unbiased best geostatistical analysis which resulted in residual and little variance. Cognitive radio in construction can find the best option in adopting locations to determine the distances between measurements and interrelation locations available through the minimum distance. Dirichlet tessellations are one of the best alternative methods used in the construction of Voronoi diagrams for detecting all locations with the same signal level.

Spectrum Sensing Techniques

Cabric, O'Donnell, Chen and Brodersen (2006) opined that the main components of cognitive radio are to study, detect, perceive and be aware of the spectrum parameters that have a direct relationship with the radio channel characteristics. Therefore, its application can interfere with the environment in the operation of users needed. The usage of parts of the spectrum clarifies that in cognitive radio, the highest authority with deserved power is the primary user of the spectrum.

Sensing of spectrum is highly paramount in cognitive radio communications which will aid the environment in yielding and detecting the spectrum spaces. According to Sahai, Hoven, and Tandra (2004), the maximum signal which must be detected at a point when a secondary operator has a brief knowledge about the primary user's signal is known as matched filter which is detected by maximising accumulated signal noise towards the receiver's signal. Matched filter arises while relating the known signal with an unknown signal which may help in detecting an unknown signal template. Application of matched filter is fervently paramount due to its less time in achieving high processing gain because of its coherent detection.

Though the danger of matched filter regarding the primary user signal is the requirement of receiver sensing, even with the availability of the primary user signal in the cognitive radios, the matched filter can result in unlimited information but less possible in the presence of little information of the primary user signal (Cabric, Mishra, & Brodersen, 2004). The cooperative spectrum connotes the required strength for the improvement of all the channels with a lesser capacity of increment due to its measurements of local spectrum sensing for detecting the availability of primary users (Ghasemi & Souq, 2005). Ganesan and Li (2005) observed that at the failure of one cognitive radio signal, other cognitive radios are still active in detecting the signal which denies the missing of any users. One of the fervent benefits is working together which aids in improving the sensing performance through the perfectly developed communication.

Cognitive Radio Application

Cognitive radio is a technological development with many potential applications for several purposes. It is sometimes referred to as the next new generation communication network due to its wide range and functions. It can be applied in:

- Solving connection problems in rural areas,
- Regulating radio frequency operations for smart phones and Internet of Things (IoT),
- Operating as distributed networks and giant wireless hotspots,
- Managing disaster (relief),
- Providing emergency networks,
- Providing leased networks,
- Traffic control,
- City and campus wide network coverage,
- Weather forecasting,
- Medical applications, and
- Outer space communication.

Cognitive Radio Challenges

Constraints as presented in Table 1 arise as a result of a lack of combined cooperation between primary users and secondary users which purposely occurs by hard prediction and estimating of the wireless channel. Meanwhile, in wireless communication, the occurrence of interference is highly common either knowingly or unknowingly due to the noise generated, which can force the detector to assumptions about the result. In a nutshell, great determination from the detectors in detecting more signals prevents their robust intention (Zetterberg, 2011).

Noise uncertainty is one of the powerful challenges of cognitive radio; therefore, this noise power is most assumed to be known by the detectors for them to set their test statistic, whereas it is sensitive to change which is the bedrock of the problem and practically it takes too many tasks to identify the exact noise power in the spectrum (Tandra & Sahai, 2005). Disrespect of rules and principles of cognitive radio spectrum by the users on the channel can result in false alarms and

Table 1. Showing Challenges of Cognitive Radio.

Author	Cognitive Radio Challenges
Zetterberg (2011)	• Lack of combined cooperation between users • interference • result assumption • detectors underperforming
Tandra and Sahai (2005)	• noise uncertainty • sensitivity to change • complex spectrum
Letaief and Zhang (2009)	• false alarm system • missing of possible detection • interference within the spectrum • delay • inconsistent results

miss detection through lack of proper utilisation of the spectrum to the fullest which may cause interference with the primary users. Moreover, the interference may affect the expected result when making amendments to the data and delay will be experienced (Letaief & Zhang, 2009).

At the point of discovering a low strength-wide area network within the spectrum, the application of cognitive radio technologies with the ability to move from one particular band to another set in productively increases the scalability of the network (Manz, 2010). The involvement of hardware requires intelligent management that can perfectly control any unexpected issues that arise when the focus is on reducing expenses with the aid of smart city applications.

Conclusion

More than a decade ago, the adoption of cognitive radio technology has been in place; spectrum radio can effectively be improved through the application of the technology. Having revealed that cooperative communication is one of the secrets behind cognitive radio success, the study expatiated on how to improve wireless devices through the application of new bands and adequate utilisation of spectrum to the fullest. This is intended to solve some issues or constraints like lack of cordial and mutual cooperation which may arise between different users of the spectrum irrespective of the challenges that might deprive the effective utilisation of cognitive radio spectrum. In construction, locations can be detected for construction to take place. This detection will come with the benefits of presenting further information about the locations and what methods to use in the project design and execution even before the commencement of the project.

References

Cabric, D., Mishra, S. M., & Brodersen, R. W. (2004). Implementation issues in spectrum sensing for cognitive radio: Record of the thirty-eight Asilomar conference. *Signals, Systems and Computers, 1*(1), 772–776.

Cabric, D., O'Donnell, I. D., Chen, M. S. W., & Brodersen, R. W. (2006). BSpectrum sharing radios. *Institute of Electrical and Electronics Engineers (IEEE) Circuits System Management, 6*(2), 30–45.

Ganesan, G., & Li, Y. G. (2005). Agility improvement through cooperation diversity in cognitive radio. In *Proceeding of Institute of Electrical and Electronics Engineers IEEE Global Telecommunication Conference (GLOBECOM)*, St. Louis, Missouri, November 28–December 2 (pp. 2505–2509).

Ghasemi, A., & Souq, E. S. (2005). Collaborative spectrum sensing for opportunistic access in fading environments. In *Proceedings of the First Institute of Electrical and Electronics Engineers (IEEE) Symposium on New frontiers Dynamics Spectrum Access Network (DySPAN)*, Baltimore, Maryland, November 8–11 (pp. 131–136).

Granelli, F. (2010). .Standardization and research in cognitive and dynamic spectrum access, networks: IEEE Scc41 efforts and other activities. *Institute of Electrical and Electronics Engineers (IEEE) Communicative Management, 48*(1), 71–79.

Han, Z., & Liu, K. J. R. (2008). *Resource allocation for wireless networks; basic, techniques and applications.* Cambridge: Cambridge University Press.

Haykin, S. (2005). Cognitive radio: Brain-empowered wireless communications. *Institute of Electrical and Electronics Engineers (IEEE) Journal of Selective Communication, 23*(3), 201–220.

Letaief, K., & Zhang, W. (2009). Cooperative communication for cognitive radio networks. *Proceedings of the Institute of Electrical and Electronics Engineers (IEEE), 97*(3), 878–893.

Manz, B. (2010). Standardizing IoT connectivity by the Kilometer: SIGFOX, KoRa, or LTE? Retrieved from http://eu.mouser.com/applications/sigfox-lora-1te/

Mitola, J., & Maguire, G. Q. (1999). Cognitive radio; making software radios more personal. *Institute of Electrical and Electronics Engineers IEEE Personal Communication, 6*(4), 13–18.

Sahai, A., Hoven, N., & Tandra, R. (2004). *Some Fundamental Limits on Cognitive Radio. Allerton Conference on Communication, Control, and Computing*, Monticello, October 21–23 (pp. 1662–1671). Retrieved from https://www.people.eecs.berkeley.edu

Shepard, D. (2014). A two-dimensional interpolation function for irregularly-spaced data. *Proceedings of 1968 23rd ACM National Conference*, New York, August 27–29 (pp. 517–524). doi:10.1145/800186.810616

Tandra, R., & Sahai, A. (2005). Fundamental limits on detection in low SNR under noise uncertainty. In *Progressing of the International Conference on Wireless Networks, Communications and Mobile Computing (WirelessCom'05)*, Maui, Hawaii, June 2005 (Vol. 1, No. 2, pp. 464–469).

Zetterberg, L. H. (2011). Signal detection under noise interference in a game situation. *IRE Transactions on information Theory, 8*(1), 47–57.

Chapter 12

Radio Frequency Identification (RFID) for Sustainable Infrastructure Management

Abstract

This chapter presented radio frequency identification (RFID) as a techno-logical gadget used in various industries to improve information and tracking equipment. The adoption of RFID in the construction industry has been scarcely used due to the dissemination of its potential to construction professionals in the industry. RFID is generally used as a wireless device that transmits information using radio waves. The benefits associated with using RFID in the construction industry were discussed along with challenges, and its functions to the construction process.

Keywords: Communication; construction reality; information communica-tion; radio communication; radio frequency; sustainable construction

Introduction

Radio Frequency Identification (RFID) is widely used in the manufacturing industry to facilitate the handling of goods and materials, especially through barcode technology. In recent times, the use of RFID has outsmarted barcode technology because it permits identification from a distance and does not require a line of sight to carry out its operations (Kaur, Sandhu, Mohan, & Sandhu, 2011). RFID was first introduced in 1945 as a sensible tool for transmitting radio waves with audio information; but now, it is viewed as an effective automatic records collection technology that is widely used in the manufacturing and logistics industries (Domdouzis, Kumar, & Anumba, 2007). The RFID reader communicates with its tag by using radio waves (Trappey et al., 2017). RFID science is a Wi-Fi sensor technological know-how based totally on the detection of electromagnetic signals used for object identification and monitoring (McCarthy, Nguyen, Rashid, & Soroczak, 2003). Even though its usage is paramount to several industries, there have been challenges experienced in its

A Digital Path to Sustainable Infrastructure Management, 111–115
Copyright © 2024 Ayodeji E. Oke and Seyi S. Stephen
Published under exclusive licence by Emerald Publishing Limited
doi:10.1108/978-1-83797-703-120241012

adoption across several industries. The major challenge is identified as cost in acquisition and replacement.

The worth of RFID in the world market (as of the year 2000) was rated to be $900 million, and between the years 2005 and 2009, it went up to $5.56 billion. This was possible due to the awareness of its usage in other industries it was anticipated to rise to $ 8.25 billion within the next few years (Li & Becerik-Gerber, 2011). Based on these data, RFID technology is an expensive gadget that can only be afforded by a few industries. The technology has also been seen as the fastest moving technology in the world, and this corroborates the upsurge in worth projection experienced over the years (Duan & Cao, 2020). The construction industry uses this technology to disseminate information throughout construction phases and also track equipment regarding mobility, repairs, operations, etc. Several industries outside the construction industry have adopted RFID technology into their operations.

The manufacturing industries, for example, have adopted RFID into their daily activities. However, there has been low compliance with RFID in the construction industry due to its cost and the scenario that some construction firms still function on manual operations in carrying out project work (Boddy, Rezgui, Cooper, & Wetherill, 2007). But as construction professionals get to look past the cost and inculcate its application in construction, RFID became more popular among other sectors of the economy (Domdouzis et al., 2007).

As previously stated, the gradual adoption of RFID in the construction industry has necessitated its growth over time. RFID involves tags or transponders that can accumulate records and control them in a portable, changeable database and communicate activities instructions (Schneider, 2004). In certain applications, it beats differently when compared to auto linear code (1D) technologies. For example, in places where vision is blocked or where surfaces appear dirty, it performs better than barcodes which are a benefit that magnetic stripes and contact buttons do not have (Forger, 1990). RFID has a read-and-write capacity which makes it different from material management and identification tag (Zhu, Mukhopadhyay, & Kurata, 2012). The rewritable tag capacity of RFID enables it to strengthen national security and improve the maintenance of service records. In addition, RFID can alert an automobile owner when there is an oil change or when another routine maintenance is required or available. It also enhances the user's potential to locate objects when used in combination with a global positioning system (GPS) for real-time (Schneider, 2004).

RFID in Construction Project

Construction projects are sometimes extraordinarily complicated and often take place in uncontrolled, unprepared and dynamic surroundings where each undertaking goes through various phases before leading to completion. Because of this, cutting-edge construction management requires real-time and correct statistics for sharing among all parties concerned to undertake efficient and high-quality planning, as well as execution of the tasks (Kini, 1999). Effective and environment-friendly first-rate management may also be needed when trying to complete tasks within the price range and deadlines. With the creation of the internet, web-based statistics administration options have facilitated statistics distribution and information sharing among individuals (Wang, 2008). This information is collected and made available through a system for all the construction parties involved regarding the project execution (Ergen & Akinci, 2007).

RFID Reality

RFID technology is a Wi-Fi sensor science which is transmitted through electromagnetic signal. It consists of a transceiver with decoder, an antenna or coil and a transponder programmed electronically with unique facts (McCarthy, O'Donnell, & O'Reilly, 2002). The primary component of RFID can be classified into active and passive RFIDs.

Active RFID

Active RFID tag requires strength supplied from either powered infrastructure or use energy saved in a built-in battery. The existing span of RFID is limited to the saved energy and the variety of operations the device must undergo. An example of RFID is a transponder tag attached to aeroplane that identifies when a plane arrives in a country (Finkelzeller, 2003).

Passive RFID

Passive RFID is an important tag which does not require batteries or maintenance. The tag has an indefinite operational life and can only be shaped into a sensible adhesive tag (Kaur et al., 2011). This tag comprises of:

- Antenna which captures the strength and transfers the tag ID,
- An antenna that is connected to a semi-conductor chip, and
- Some shape of encapsulation which maintains the tag integrity and protects the antenna.

Benefits of RFID

RFID gadget is tailored to control materials, product flows and growth in the building industry, such as concrete, pipework, earthwork, structural steel works and curtain walls (Jaselskis & El-Misalami, 2003). RFID research has been based completely on records accumulated using RFID technology. Thus, it can be utilised to develop management and size for gathering the required data. Further benefits of RFID application in construction are:

- It provides ease in commination,
- For object identification and monitoring,

- Accumulation of records and control,
- Object location when combined with GPS, and
- Gathers data and keep records.

Conclusion

The reason why RFID has not been fully implemented by the construction professionals in the built industry despite its numerous benefits is majorly its cost implication. However, its level of awareness is another identified challenge exercised by construction professionals, especially in developing countries. RFID is adopted in the construction industry to track and locate materials and to break the barriers to information dissemination. The information obtained from RFID can be used to improve supply chain efficiency and offer huge advantages to operations in several industries. So, RFID is a gifted technology for the construction industry to promote cost control, identify vehicles and track materials.

References

Boddy, S., Rezgui, Y., Cooper, G., & Wetherill, M. (2007). Computer integrated construction: A review and proposals for future direction. *Advances in Engineering Software, 38*(10), 677–687.

Domdouzis, K., Kumar, B., & Anumba, C. (2007). Radio-Frequency Identification (RFID) applications: A brief introduction. *Advanced Engineering Informatics, 21*(4), 350–355.

Duan, K. K., & Cao, S. Y. (2020). Emerging RFID technology in structural engineering – A review. *Structures, 4*(28), 2404–2414.

Ergen, E., & Akinci, B. (2007). *An overview of approaches for utilizing RFID in construction industry.* Retrieved from https://www.ieeexplore.ieee.org

Finkelzeller, K. (2003). *The RFID handbook* (2nd ed.). Chichester: John Wiley and Sons.

Forger, G. (1990). Automatic identification: Its role in the 90's. *Modern Materials Handling, 45*(2), 57–61.

Jaselskis, E. J., & El-Misalami, T. (2003). Implementing radio frequency identification in the construction process. *Journal of Construction Engineering and Management, 129*(6), 680–688.

Kaur, M., Sandhu, M., Mohan, N., & Sandhu, P. S. (2011). RFID technology principles, advantages, limitations and its applications. *International Journal of Computer and Electrical Engineering, 3*(1), 151–174.

Kini, D. U. (1999). Materials management: The key to successful project management. *Journal of Management in Engineering, 15*(1), 30–34.

Li, N., & Becerik-Gerber, B. (2011). Life-cycle approach for implementing RFID technology in construction: Learning from academic and industry use cases. *Journal of Construction Engineering and Management, 137*(12), 1089–1098.

McCarthy, J. F., Nguyen, D. H., Rashid, A. M., & Soroczak, S. (2003). Proactive displays and the experience UbiComp project. *ACM SIGGROUP Bulletin, 23*(3), 38–41.

McCarthy, J., O'Donnell, P., & O'Reilly, P. (2002). RFID systems and security and privacy implications. *Computer Science, 25*(23), 454–469. doi:10.1007/3-540-36400-5_332

Schneider, M. (2004). *Radio Frequency Identification (RFID) technology and its applications in the commercial construction industry.* Retrieved from https://www.e-pub.uni-weimar.de

Trappey, A. J., Trappey, V. C., Fan, C. Y., Hsu, A. P., Li, X. K., & Lee, I. J. (2017). IoT patent roadmap for smart logistic service provision in the context of Industry 4.0. *Journal of the Chinese Institute of Engineers, 40*(7), 593–602.

Wang, L. C. (2008). Enhancing construction quality inspection and management using RFID technology. *Automation in Construction, 17*(4), 467–479.

Zhu, X., Mukhopadhyay, S. K., & Kurata, H. (2012). A review of RFID technology and its managerial applications in different industries. *Journal of Engineering and Technology Management, 29*(1), 152–167.

Chapter 13

Cyber Technology for Sustainable Infrastructure Management

Abstract

In the effort to procure solutions to emerging challenges faced in the construction industry, construction stakeholders implemented the use of several technologies in construction operations from the onset of project planning to completion. Cyber technology introduced into construction brought about the inclusion of wearable technology, mobile devices, apps, project management software, drones, 3D printers, robotics, etc. to enhance output as the industry tends towards that which is sustainable. This chapter identified benefits, barriers and other related cyber technology interactions within the scope of delivering projects that are of standard, budget and quality at the same time. The conclusion gave a summary of the whole chapter for further comprehension.

Keywords: Device integration; digital construction; project delivery; project success; sustainable construction; sustainable resources

Introduction

Cyber technology refers to electronic devices specifically on nearly formed media (including virtual reality (VR), multimedia and convivial events) used for visible information gathering, soft computing and mobile computing. Sustainable construction has been touted as the remedy to infrastructural building challenges, in achieving a healthy environment created on environmental conduct. Cyber technology for sustainable construction deals with the use of electronic devices, specifically emerging technologies for information gathering, mobile and soft computing, combating challenges about infrastructural development and building projects to achieve enhanced project delivery through sound climate practice dependent on environmental laws and guidelines (Gunes, Pefers, Givargis, & Vahid, 2014).

A Digital Path to Sustainable Infrastructure Management, 117–124
Copyright © 2024 Ayodeji E. Oke and Seyi S. Stephen
Published under exclusive licence by Emerald Publishing Limited
doi:10.1108/978-1-83797-703-120241013

As technologies are incessantly being used across industries for different purposes, the construction industry cannot relax on already adopted technological practices. This stretch to the fact that sectors in the economy have massively moved towards digital operations and the construction industry must match this paradigm shift to meet the demands and expectations expected of the industry. In addition, sustainability is easily achieved through the adoption of technological practices and innovations in further construction activities through the engagement of new technologies either as an upgrade or new ones formulated within the concept of achieving green construction. Some of the devices associated with cyber technology are:

- Wearable technology,
- 3D printers,
- Drones,
- Robotics,
- Sensors,
- Actuators,
- Smart phones,
- Smart machines, etc.

(Gunes et al., 2014)

Digitalisation in Construction

The construction sector contributes significantly to the overall economic development of any nation. The industry achieved this by revamping diverse available means into constructed social and economic infrastructures and its output is necessary for other industries as well (Ayodele & Alabi, 2011). Even with its importance, construction industries in some nations have been affected by bad implementation in carrying out operations mostly through redundancy towards digital participation in the construction process (Sezer, Thunberg, & Wernicke, 2021).

With no form of remorse, any construction industry that refuses to work towards technological acceptance and infusion into construction activities will suffer hardship in the quest for the digitalisation of construction exercise. Unnikrishnan, Manjunatha, and Negenda (2016) and Aghimien Aigbavboa, Oke, and Thwala (2020) indicated that digital transfiguration can be challenging to achieve if there are no economic and professional capabilities in place. To kerb this undesirable situation, Aghimien et al. (2020) stated that collaboration with other firms or industries with similar objectives and the same dreams will help in the digital transformation and transfiguration of the construction industry.

Study shows that construction organisations that use more technology thrive and leads in digital transformations than other companies that do not. Modern technologies like artificial intelligence (AI), VR, robotics, augmented reality (AR) and so on are being used by some of these digitally transformed industries across the globe with more reference to the developed nations in achieving operations and functionalities.

Cyber Technology in Construction

Cyber technology is not idle on its own; it is integrated with existing technologies or technologies that are presently developed for its function. Cyber technology is supported by several other technologies classified into two types according to their level of implementation. The first is technologies currently accepted and implemented in the architecture engineering and construction (AEC) industry such as global positioning system (GPS), building information processing (BIM), drones, portable devices and image-capturing technologies that are popularly employed in the construction process in both developed and developing countries (Akanmu, Anumba, & Messener, 2013). These technologies can support higher level cyber technology integration for more advanced functions as well as implementation. The second type is technologies that are still in development. These technologies are not fully incorporated into construction activities even though the level of awareness has improved over the years (Linares, Anumba, & Esfahan, 2019). Examples are AI, robotics, the Internet of Things (IoT), AR, VR, etc. Irrespective of the groups where these technologies are categorised, incorporation with cyber technology is directed towards:

- Project enhancement,
- Project delivery,
- Swift completion of construction,
- Profit maximisation,
- Security,
- Sustainable development,
- Green construction,
- Efficiency and project quality, etc.

Enabling Technologies

The technologies that allow for the integration of coordination (in double) between virtual and the real construction are listed below:

- Virtual prototyping,
- Wireless sensors, and
- Communication networks.

Drivers of Cyber Technology Application in Construction

There are several emerging innovations presently used in modern construction. Examples of these technologies are the IoT, cloud computing, robotics, big data, building information modelling, and man-made intelligence, etc. which have access to all levels of construction life span.

The identification of the implementation of technology in construction popularly referred to as the Fourth Industrial Revolution (Industry 4.0) is rebranding the construction sector and metamorphosing it into that which is not only smart, but also functional in terms of project planning, execution and delivery within sustainable means as shown in Fig. 1 below.

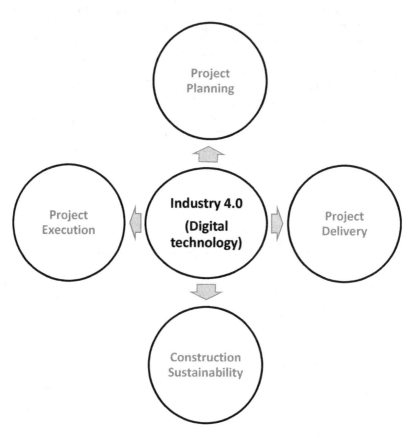

Fig. 1.   Functional Construction Through the Implementation of Digital Technology.

The responsibility of driving cyber technology applications for sustainable construction lies on all partners in the development business and not only on the professionals alone. Already, new technologies have evolved for producing designs and preparing estimates within a short period. Professionals in construction are continually seeking alternate concepts for the sustainability of products in the industry.

Challenges of Cyber Technology in Construction

Challenges related to cyber technology implementation are identified below:

- Software vulnerabilities,
- Cloud attacks,
- Privacy,
- Device learning and artificial learning attacks,
- Insider attack,
- Policies (government, regulatory, individual, etc.),
- Cost of implementation and running,
- Size of project,
- Nature of project work,
- Redundant attitude towards technology,
- Inadequate skilled personnel, etc.

(Esterle & Grosu, 2016)

In terms of software vulnerabilities, some advanced software is vulnerable to minimal cyberattacks. But in most cases, the majority of the technologies attached to cyber technology are susceptible to external threats. And this has contributed to most of the challenges experienced in the use of technology as a solution-driven channel in many industries. Cyber technology is not solely affected by this, coupled with other challenging factors that have contributed to the slow adoption of technology in general practice. Some of these challenges are expatiated below.

Machine Learning (ML) and AI Attacks

Despite the advantages embedded in the applications of ML and AI which have brought about tremendous growth in different industries, it has however endangered some operations to attacks. For example, unscrupulous individuals tend to launch attacks on coding in ML and AI which makes the systems to be open to risks and thus subsequently affects economic transactions and technological functions they are brought in for.

Bring Your Own Device (BYOD) Policy

In the system that operates a BYOD policy, there is a possibility of an individual (employee or employer) hacking into the system to get or access vital information regarding the project. This can easily be facilitated when the device is outdated and the firewall has become pervious for the external unwanted party with little or no restriction. Since cyber technology is somewhat dependent on already existing technologies, there is a possibility of this happening even without the operators knowing such an act has been committed on the system (Sheth, Anantharam, & Henson, 2013). Information hacked can result in several accounted or unaccounted problems that will affect project delivery and the whole life cycle.

Possible Unemployment

The construction industry is one of the most employers of labour due to the enormous work and tasks involved in it. However, with the invention of cyber technology or technology in general, there is the possibility of the employees being laid off since lesser manpower is required to control devices. And with some of the construction industries moving towards technological-driven operations, traditional procurement methods will fizzle out in time and this will lead to some services (skilled and unskilled) not being required much like before the adoption of an information and communication technology (ICT)-related industry.

Benefits of Cyber Technology for Construction Project

Cyber technology in recent time is changing increasingly at a rapid stride aiding in daily production and empirical functions. In construction, cyber technology can be beneficial in terms of:

- Materials optimisation,
- Budgeting,
- Improved site safety,
- Resources management,
- Waste management,
- Daily remote management,
- Reducing insurance premium,
- Increased efficiency,
- Remote management, etc.

(Sezer et al., 2021)

How Cyber Technology Is Changing Construction

Cyber technology with numerous electronic devices emerging in today's world is changing and bringing benefits to the construction industry through the following devices:

Wearable Technology

The concept of wearable technology is that which encompasses reality through different automated means. Examples are recognised in the usage of a covered vest integrated with a GPS and radio that detects and warn the user as it nears a risky area. Also, there is a harrow hard hat that can process third-generation (3D) images through integrated AR. These technologies have improved safety on construction sites and hence improve construction delivery within the safest possible situation.

Mobile Devices, Applications and Project Management Software

Concerning benefits in communication, collaboration and coordination of doff rent construction elements; building information modelling (BIM) is a software that has a huge influence on how construction is viewed these days, especially in some construction industries that have limited advanced technologies such as AI, robotics, etc. These devices, applications and software have been able to improve and substitute several construction designs, plans, executions, management, etc. even from reconnaissance to completion. Not only this, construction professionals have become more efficient through the usage of these platforms in carrying out the construction process.

Drones

This gathers data from different environments for analysis and interpretation to make decisions based on the information collected. Drones also help in site guarding, inspections and general assessments of a construction site irrespective of operations without many problems. Drones can either be manned or unmanned depending on the capacity and function of the designated device. Also, drones follow up on logistics, labour force and discharge of materials on site.

Robotics

Robots can carry out different levels of assignment like demolition, excavation and bricklaying with observations and in lesser time. They can be strictly controlled remotely, irrespective of the location or environment. Robotic functions are self-sufficient thus lowering risks that staff and workers are exposed to on construction sites.

Conclusion

Having highlighted the process of cyber technology for sustainable construction, how it works, challenges, benefits and devices used to carry out virtual models, along with other subsections of this chapter, it can thus be asserted that cyber technology implementation into constriction practice will propel the industry to that which is more advanced and sustainable. Therefore, cyber technology for sustainable construction should be encouraged as it is carried out with environmental policies for intended sustainable developmental goals.

References

Aghimien, D. O., Aigbavboa, C., Oke, A. E., & Thwala, W. D. (2020). Digitalization of construction organizations – A case for digital partnering. *International Journal of Construction Management*, 22(3), 1–10. doi:10.1080/15623599.2020.1745134

Akanmu, A., Anumba, C., & Messener, J. (2013). Scenarios for cyber-physical system integration in construction. *Journal of Information Technology in Construction, 18*(12), 240–260.

Ayodele, E. O., & Alabi, O. M. (2011). Abandonment of construction projects in Nigeria: Causes and effects. *Journal of Emerging Trends in Economics and Management Science (JETEMS), 2*(2), 142–145.

Esterle, L., & Grosu. (2016). Cyber-physical systems: Challenge of the 21st century. *Elektrotechnik and informationstechnik, 133*(7), 299–303.

Gunes, V., Pefers, S., Givargis, T., & Vahid, F. (2014). A survey on concepts, application, and challenges in cyber-physical systems. *Transaction on Internet and Information Systems (TIIS), 8*(12), 4242–4268.

Linares, D. A., Anumba, C., & Esfahan, N. R. (2019). Overview of supporting technologies for cyber physical systems implementation in the AEC industry. *Computing in Civil Engineering, 1*(1), 495–504.

Sezer, A. A., Thunberg, M., & Wernicke, B. (2021). Digitalization index: Developing a model for assessing the degree of digitalization of construction projects. *Journal of Construction Management, 147*(10), 0402–1119.

Sheth, A., Anantharam, P., & Henson, C. (2013). Physical-cyber-social computing; an early 21st century approach. *Institute of Electrical and Electronics Engineers (IEEE) Intelligent Systems, 28*(1), 78–82.

Unnikrishnan, H., Manjunatha, B., & Negenda, H. (2016). Contested urban commons: Mapping the transition of a lake to a sports stadium in Bangalore. *International Journal of the Commons, 10*(1), 1–25. Retrieved from https://www.thecommonsjournal.org

Chapter 14

Mechatronics for Sustainable Infrastructure Management

Abstract

The world is becoming digitised, and the construction industry is not left behind in the move. Buildings are getting advanced to the level of operating them electronically with little or no human interference. The implementation of technological practices into operations has produced many new products and provided ways of improving the efficiency of the products. A practical example is the application of robots being involved in the construction process. And these robotics are controlled by the use of mechatronics engineering through their artificial intelligence incorporated into their systems. This chapter examined the activities and involvement of mechatronics in construction, the different benefits to be derived from mechatronics applications and the uphill challenges it poses in construction projects.

Keywords: Digital construction; digital technology; modern technology; project delivery; robotic construction; sustainable construction

Introduction

Intelligent building systems are on the rise in the last decades; these intelligent building systems involve the use of applied technology information, control of the energy supply and lighting technology information, security control system information, fire-alarm and firefighting information, the control of doors and windows, automatic condition display control used in many modern household appliances and buildings are facilitated by the implementation of mechatronic technologies (Dudas & Toth, 2016).

In the application of mechatronics, it comes in play across several areas. The use of this technology for carrying out specified purposes are incorporated for functions in the following areas:

A Digital Path to Sustainable Infrastructure Management, 125–131

Copyright © 2024 Ayodeji E. Oke and Seyi S. Stephen

Published under exclusive licence by Emerald Publishing Limited

doi:10.1108/978-1-83797-703-120241014

- Automation of machines,
- Biomedical systems,
- Computer aided design (CAD),
- Computer numerical control (CNC),
- Data communication systems,
- Direct numerical control,
- Energy and power systems,
- Industrial goods,
- Servo-mechanics, and
- Vehicular systems among others.

(Akele, Okoh, Ejiofor, & Alimasunya, 2011)

Evolution of Mechatronics Engineering

The word 'Mechatronics' is the combination of 'Mechanical' and 'Electronics', but in the real sense of it, mechatronics involves the integration of electronics, mechanical, computer, electrical, telecommunications, products, robotics and control engineering into desired functions as illustrated in figure and Table 1. Also, the use of artificial intelligence (AI) in all fields is a direct product of mechatronics engineering not limited to just mechanical and electronics engineering. According to Maki (2007), mechatronics represents the unification of interdisciplinary intelligence coupled with adaptive engineering and technology. Mechatronics was first mentioned by Tetsuro Mori, a Japanese Engineer, in 1969. At first, mechatronics was not internally popular until after the 1980s as more professionals referenced its benefits in the field of mechanical and electronics engineering (Alciatore & Histand, 2015). Before the introduction of mechatronics, most appliances operated on mechanical modules without the use of sensors, with

Table 1. The Interpretation of Several Practices Integrated Into Mechatronics.

Code	Meaning
MCH	Mechanical
ECT	Electronics
COM	Computer
ELT	Electrical
TCM	Telecommunications
PRD	Products
RBT	Robotics
CTE	Control engineering

further breakthroughs in engineering necessitating the need for mechatronics in several aspects of human development (Hehenberger & Bradley, 2016).

Since the implementation of mechatronics in several related fields, controlling machines became easier and simpler due to the functional aspect of the technology incorporated into machine systems. This gave the platform for easy navigation and incorporation into both computer software and hardware. Also, functionality was maximised in terms of product delivery. Irrespective of the size or capacity of the product, the configuration was done within budget without reducing quality and quantity. Even though the technology has been around for a while now, its adoption into further practices was not really into action until now when industries and individuals are fully acquainted with using the term in practice (Fig. 1).

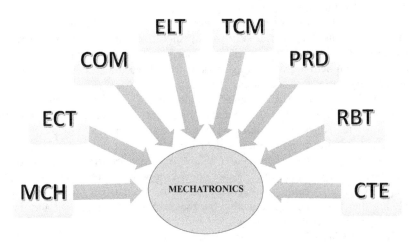

Fig. 1.   The Integration of Several Practices Into Mechatronics.

Mechatronics in Construction Projects

Construction industries have not been left behind in the integration of mechatronics into their activities. The involvement of mechatronics spans off-site (pre-construction) fabrications, on-site installations and post-construction activities as opined by Delgado et al. (2019). The areas of integration of mechatronics in construction include inter alia:

3D Printing and Robotics: The invention of the automated machine to enable 3D printing of components of the construction project has helped the fabrication of the building. Construction works can now be done with accuracy and precision with these printings showing details that might have been neglected before. Whereas robotics can be deployed on-site to help with installation, supervision, monitoring, surveillance, etc. (Delgado et al., 2019).

Automated Construction System: Processes like welding, materials handling, cutting, bricks laying, etc. can be done with little or no man involvement due to automated machines invented with the use of mechatronics technology. Nearly, all the activities that were used to be done manually can now be successfully automated with little or no effort whatsoever.

Controlled Demolition: In a populated area, demolition is now done by the use of mechatronics devices, thereby eliminating the fear of damages to adjourning properties and injury to persons. This in turn saves costs that might arise in terms of litigation and the like.

Autonomous Vehicles: Autonomous vehicles have succeeded in unmanned autonomous pile loading operations as an example. Arai (2012) stated that in the development of an Odometer; path planning and following, along with required travelling control can now be successfully measured accurately to get a precise geometric path. Also, an autonomous excavator can be used in areas where it is dangerous for humans to navigate.

Drones: This is one of the mechatronics devices used in the construction industry. It is used for aerial surveys and monitoring/inspection of site work. Delgado et al. (2019) in their study mentioned that the combination of vehicles and drones can help in transporting workers from hazardous environments (sites) while taking samples of such areas at the same time.

Lean Construction: Mechatronics engineering has made lean construction a more sustainable one. The deployment of mechatronics technology eliminates waste on site. Aloes have improved construction efficiency through different automated systems integrated into construction activities.

Automated Building Component Operations: Sensor-controlled doors, gates, windows, sanitary appliances, etc. are some components. The control of these components is now made possible with the use of mechatronics technology. Not only are they operated electronically, but they can also be monitored and that is advantageous in terms of security.

Safety and Security Monitoring Devices: Movement sensing devices for both on-site construction activities and post-construction activities are now in use. Also, automatic heat humidifiers and smoke detectors are safety devices that are made possible through the use of mechatronics technology.

Benefits of Mechatronics in Construction Projects

Accuracy and Precisions

With the use of mechatronics devices on site, the issue of accuracy and precision in measuring items and assembling construction parts can be achieved with lesser stress. This is unlike before when human errors find their way into such measurements and thus make them void of accuracy.

High-Quality Productions

The quality of the end product of construction activities has greatly improved with the introduction of mechatronics technology into it. Quality of works on structures, composite items and finishes is on the increase due to these inventions.

Time Saving

Time used in construction activities on site has improved. The construction completion duration is lesser now when compared to/what was obtainable before. We are in an era where multi-storey buildings can be erected in a matter of weeks and not in years.

Minimising Financial Loss

Inclement weather is one of the major challenges in construction which always results in financial loss. But with the introduction of the mechatronics engineering system, such damages have been reduced because more precise methods and practices have been developed over time. Also, since construction duration is completed faster with the implementation of mechatronics, the direct result of this will be experienced in the reduced project budget.

Reduction of Wastes

Lean construction that is made more achievable through mechatronics in construction projects enables the reduction of waste throughout the construction process. This is beneficiary to the construction industry as it moves towards sustainability.

Challenges of Mechatronics in Construction Projects

Integration of mechatronics into construction is not without its challenges. These uphill challenges have limited the level of its usage in the construction industry and even in almost every other fields. These challenges are:

- *Cost of acquiring mechatronics equipment by contractors* – The economy of most contractors cannot still accommodate the acquisition of these devices, even though they wish to integrate them into their activities. This is because of its huge initial capital outlay and the construction industry being a low-profit and high-risk one (Delgado et al., 2019). Particularly, in developing countries where the economy is still struggling to survive, most contractors could not afford this mechatronics equipment.
- *Client inability to pay for its service* – In situations where contractors can acquire these devices to be used, the client economy in most cases cannot accommodate it. The fear that the initial cost will overrun makes some clients

decline its usage. This challenge is compounded by the policy of selecting the 'lowest' bid for the award of a contract which limits the involvement of innovation since the contractor would not want to lose at the end of the day (Delgado et al., 2019).

- *Lack of technical know-how* – Technically, some are still lacking behind on the usage of these devices in construction projects. Most of the workforce in the construction industry lacks basic training on the usage and interaction of these mechatronics devices. So, deploying them to activities will be difficult as few skilled personnel would be available to manage them.
- *Lack of improvising* – Part of the challenges of integrating mechatronics into a construction project is the singularity of functions in which most of these devices are programmed. Unlike humans that can function across phases when the need arises, some of these devices still need to be controlled by humans. In robot and autonomous vehicles, for example, once the button is pressed, the instruction code in the form of AI is deployed and followed strictly with no improvisation expected.

Conclusion

The evolution of mechatronics has developed industries across several disciplines over the years. Through its integration of mechanical and electronic features, a paradigm shift has been experienced in what engineering science was to that which is presently practiced interdisciplinary. Also, it has opened channels for the discovery of new fields capable of fostering the world into a sustainable one through the stimulation of synergy, fusion and interdisciplinary efforts put together towards the built industry and also other science, technology, engineering and mathematics industries. Despite the promising benefits and enhancement in mechatronics, its level of adoption is considerably low in most countries. It will be beneficial if its implementation and adoption are more publicised, especially to the stakeholders and the professionals in the construction industry.

References

Akele, S. M. G., Okoh, H. C. V., Ejiofor, V., & Alimasunya, E. (2011). Mechatronics automobiles and the roadside auto-mechanics: Challenges and vision 20:2020. In *Auchi: The 1st International Conference on Engineering and Technology (ICET 2011)*, School of Engineering, Auchi Polytechnic, Auchi, Nigeria.

Alciatore, D., & Histand, M. (2015). *Introduction to mechatronics and measurement systems* (3rd ed.). New York, NY: McGraw-Hill Higher Education.

Arai, T. (2012). *Advanced robotics and mechatronics and their applications in construction automation.* Osaka: Department of Systems Innovation, School of Engineering Science, Osaka University.

Delgado, J. M., Oyedele, L., Ajayi, A., Akanbi, L., Akinade, O., Bilal, M., & Owolabi, H. (2019). Robotics and automated systems in construction:

Understanding industry specific challenges for adoption. *Journal of Building Engineering*, 5(4), 1183–1188.

Dudas, E., & Toth, N. (2016). *Building Mechatronics as the device of improving energy efficiency in intelligent buildings*. Retrieved from https://www.citeseerx.ist.psu.edu

Hehenberger, P., & Bradley, D. (2016). *Mechatronic futures: Challenges and solutions for mechatronic systems and their designers*. Cham: Springer. doi:10.1007/978-3-319-32156-1

Maki, K. H. (2007). Mechatronics a unifying interdisciplinary and intelligent engineering science paradigm: Summer 2007. *Industrial Electronics Magazine*, 1(1), 12–24.

Chapter 15

Digital Twin for Sustainable Infrastructure Management

Abstract

This chapter discussed the implementation of the digital twin (DT) idea into construction. Through the adoption of DTs into construction practices, construction professionals have been able to project an identical virtual concept of sections of the project execution right from the onset. In the introduction and discussing of its origin, the DT was further assessed about its applications in construction beneficial in enhancing project delivery. Other sections like barriers, drivers and benefits of the DT in construction summarised what this chapter represents in terms of discussing the new involvement of digital tools in construction execution, management and sustainability.

Keywords: Construction trends; construction digitalisation; digital construction; digital infrastructure; project delivery; sustainability

Introduction

The digitalisation of the construction industry has astronomical potential for suddenly enhancing the industry's practices. But in some countries (mostly developing) especially in regards to current measures in construction project management, the industry continues to be dependent mostly on traditional construction methods. Furthermore, the employment of absolute computerised strategies within the construction industry has not yet been a widespread practice; this may clarify why there is a gradual adoption of digital growth within the construction industry, specifically in developing countries (Abdel-Rahman et al., 2020).

To obtain a better service delivery, digitalisation utilisation in construction is defined as the innovative use of digital technologies in total service within construction practices. Consequently, digitalisation is the successful application of

A Digital Path to Sustainable Infrastructure Management, 133–140
Copyright © 2024 Ayodeji E. Oke and Seyi S. Stephen
Published under exclusive licence by Emerald Publishing Limited
doi:10.1108/978-1-83797-703-120241015

technological devices that allows it to improve day-to-day activities as well as other industries around us (Aighimien, Aigbavboa, Oke, & Thwala, 2020).

The term 'digital twin (DT)' is now frequently used in construction because of its ability to provide wider and faster access to understandable and integrated information. A DT is not just a tool, but also a set of procedures that can aid the transformation construction industry, which has remained unchanged for years (Kaewunruen, Rungskunroch, & Welsh, 2018).

In addition to the diversity of DTs, Okeagu and Mgbemena (2020) indicated that it has been engaged in other fields especially when accuracy is expected from the equipment concerning digital models for predictive maintenance. These benefits have been seen in capital-intensive equipment such as cars, jet engines, robots and other automatically oriented machines especially when performance and improvement are critical in terms of saving cost and reliability. Schleich, Anwer, Mathieu, and Wartzack (2017) concluded that in meeting the demands of today's competitive market, virtual product models (DTs) have been developed and used to enhance service and product quality performance.

The Origin and Evolution of the Digital Twin (DT)

During the industrial revolution, artisans created physical objects, resulting in one-of-a-kind examples of a particular template. As a result, when the concept of interchangeable components was introduced in the 18th century, it altered the way products were fabricated and manufactured. This is the outcome of companies attempting to mass-produce duplicates of their products. As a result, mass customisation evolved, to combine two proven manufacturing techniques to produce cheap unit costs for customised products (Schleich et al., 2017).

Although, during a seminar on product lifecycle management at the University of Michigan in 2003, Michael Grieves is credited with being the first to use the word DT(Grieves, 2014). Since then, several meanings have emerged and has it spread across fields and practices. The definitions were created based on the situations in which the concept of DTs was used (Wagner et al., 2019). Grieves gave the first description of DTs as physical components, products or systems in physical space, with virtual representations in digital space and the information flowing between the two spaces (Tao, Sui, et al., 2019).

The DT has also been referred to as a mirror (reflections or virtual replica) of physical systems that characterise their real-time behaviour (Rosen, Wichert, Lo, & Bettenhausen, 2015; Tharma, Winter, & Eigner, 2019). By defining the DT as an integrated multi-physics, multi-scale, probabilistic simulation of an as-built vehicle or system that uses the best available physical models, sensor updates and fleet history, Glaessgen and Stargel (2012) expanded Rosen and Grieve's definitions to include a detailed process of achieving DTs for space vehicles. In an attempt to meet the real-time control requirements of Industry 4.0, Vatn (2018) advised that DTs should be capable to predict the response of physical systems to uncertainties. As such, Vatn (2018) further defined the DT as a digital reproduction of physical assets approaches, and systems that can be used in real-time for control and decision purposes. To improve the predicting capabilities, DTs will need to be updated over time with data provided by sensors installed on the physical system.

Rosen et al. (2015) in their study further explained that despite the manufacturing paradigms that gave rise to the duplication of products or components particularly in large amounts, the output of the manufactured duplicates was mostly not related. However, the concept of a 'twin' is creating duplicates of products or components with functions in identifying other alternatives (instances) of related products without missing out on the original goal/design among the duplicates formulated.

The advancements in simulation technology, as well as the expanding capabilities for receiving and transmitting data from products, enabled the creation of a virtual twin of physical products, making the concept of the 'DT' creative and foresighted industries especially that of construction (Glaessgen & Stargel, 2012).

Application of DT in Construction

The concept of DT is gradually implemented in construction. Through study by Kan and Anumba (2019), research opportunities and applications of DT were reviewed in construction. The concept was deemed important in construction:

- Project life cycle,
- Design,
- Execution,
- Operations, and
- Maintenance phases.

Further essentialities of DT in construction were discussed by Boje, Guerriero, Kubicki, and Rezgui (2020) and Wang, Deng, Shen, Hu, and Qi (2022) where framework was developed for extending building information modelling (BIM) into the concept. Several technologies and techniques such as sensors, simulation models and artificial intelligence, were proposed as instrumental for enhancing the capabilities of BIM as a DT of facilities in construction:

- Logistic,
- Planning,
- Supply chain management, and
- Work enhancement.

Other applications of DT in construction are listed below:

- As a framework for decreasing musculoskeletal injuries among construction professionals: The system analyses the kinematics of workers' body segments, evaluates their ergonomic exposures and conveys ergonomic hazards in an actionable way via an augmented virtual replica in the worker's field of view (Akanmu, Olayiwola, Ogunseiju, & Mcfeeters, 2020).

- In the operations and maintenance phase, DT has been applied in facility management (Xie, Lu, Parlikad, & Schooling, 2020).
- In the preventive maintenance of historical buildings (Angjeliu, Coronelli, & Cardani, 2020).
- In the bid to enhance anomaly detection within building systems, the Centre for Digital Built Britain (CDBB) proposed a national digital twin (NDT) that is more complex, diverse and data-intensive than DT that allows for a more integrated and secure built environment (Lamb, 2019).
- Xie et al. (2020) proposed a DT system that integrates diverse data sources from building components. The framework uses Bayesian algorithm to seeking instances when there are changes in patterns of sensed data and illustrates differences between regular operations and actual anomalies. Qualitative data from visual assessments of building elements and quantitative data from structural health monitoring sensors (e.g. accelerometers and displacement transducers) describing the overall performance of historical buildings are collected and represented in the corresponding virtual structure to be viewed in virtual reality (VR).

Drivers of DT in Construction

The major drivers in the implementation and adoption of DT in construction have been identified by various researchers as stated below:

- The need to estimate the remaining useful life of manufacturing equipment (Ding, Chan, Zhang, Zhou, & Zhang, 2019; Zhang, Zhang, & Yan, 2019),
- The need to reduce construction cost through execution of predictive maintenance or smart fault prediction (Gao, Lv, Hou, Liu, & Xu, 2019; Talkhestani et al., 2019),
- The need to better identify the origins and details of machine/equipment failures (Kabaldin, Shatagin, Anosov, Kolchin, & Kuz'mishina, 2019; Wang, Ye, Gao, Li, & Zhang, 2019),
- The need for quality enhancement through product quality prediction capabilities (Talkhestani et al., 2019),
- The need for productivity improvement (Ramu et al., 2022),
- The essentiality of internal process improvement initiatives: cost-cutting, productivity and quality-improvement applications (Tao, Qi, Wang, & Nee, 2019);
- The need for transparency (Zhang et al., 2019),
- Employee training (through virtual models) and safety (Gao et al., 2019), and
- The basic necessity for real-time monitoring of the physical system (Wu et al., 2019).

Barriers of DT in Construction

As much as there are several drivers and applications of DT in construction, barriers to its adoption are also not negligible. These barriers come in the forms stated below:

- Lack of maturity of prescriptive analytics approach since digital transformation projects are highly complex, and require a step-by-step implementation that may take several years.
- Process integration in information technology (IT) enabled infrastructure.
- Issues of standardisation process.
- Lack of a defined project route.
- Lack of worker's credential to DT process.
- Professionals' attitude towards change.
- Difficulty in measuring the potential advantages of DT initiatives.
- Data protection regulation.
- Cost of implementation.
- Complexity (nature and size) of the project.
- Limited standards for enabling interoperability between design platforms and information models (Gao et al., 2019; Ramu et al., 2022).

Benefits of DT in Construction

The following benefits are stated in the study by Oracle (2019). These are:

- Real-time remote monitoring and control,
- Greater efficiency and safety,
- Predictive maintenance and scheduling,
- Scenario and risk assessment,
- Better intra- and inter-team synergy and collaborations,
- More efficient and informed decision support system,
- Personalisation of products and services, and
- Better documentation and communication.

Conclusion

Firstly, a complete DT is needed for achieving acceptable accuracy in the next-generation DTs application in construction. Such information models from the completed DT will illustrate the semantics of any relationships, rules and constraints from data that are critical for understanding the behaviour of physical systems and projects. This is a necessary ingredient for the implementation of the next-generation DT applications in sustainable construction. Secondly, as DT can evolve due to changes in the state of the corresponding physical component or system, there is a need for guidelines in defining and managing the different versions. The stages at which the versions should be captured, stored and integrated should be defined. This is significant for effectively managing the DT models hence continuous effectiveness in project execution. Thirdly, data communication latency between DTs and the physical component/system is critical for achieving timely decision-making and could be application-dependent. However, there is currently no established guideline for data communication latency in construction applications. For example, stringent communication latency will be required for applications where workers need to be informed of their unsafe postures while performing work so that they can quickly self-manage their exposures, whereas a more flexible latency may be acceptable during the generation of models for long-time learning of data patterns. Fourthly, data obtained from physical components that are stored and analysed could affect data communication latency and processing costs. Finally, once DT is well embedded into construction and its challenges adequately solved/managed, the subsequent benefits will be enormous as construction strives towards continuous efficiency and improved whole life cycle.

References

Abdel-Rahman, A., Becker, A. T., Biediger, D. E., Cheung, K. C., Fekete, S. P., Gershnfeld, N. A., ... Yannuzzi, M. (2020). Space Ants: Constructing and reconfiguring large-scale structures with finite automata (media exposition). Retrieved from https://www.par.nsf.gov

Aighimien, D. O., Aigbavboa, C., Oke, A. E., & Thwala, W. D. (2020). Digitalization of construction organizations-a case for digital partnering. *International Journal of Construction Management, 22*(3), 1–10. doi:10.1080/15623599.2020.1745134

Akanmu, A. A., Olayiwola, J., Ogunseiju, O., & Mcfeeters, D. (2020). Cyber-physical postural training system for construction workers. *Automation in Construction, 117*(1), 1–12. doi:10.1016/j.autcon.2020.103272

Angjeliu, G., Coronelli, D., & Cardani, G. (2020). Development of the simulation model for Digital Twin applications in historical masonry buildings: The integration between numerical and experimental reality. *Computers & Structures, 238*(3), 106–282.

Boje, C., Guerriero, A., Kubicki, S., & Rezgui, Y. (2020). Towards a schematic Construction Digital Twin: Directions for future research. *Automation in Construction, 114*(1), 1–16. doi:10.1016/j.autcon.2020.103179

Ding, K., Chan, F. T. S., Zhang, X., Zhou, G., & Zhang, F. (2019). Defining a digital twin-based cyber-physical production system for autonomous manufacturing in smart shop floors. *International Journal of Production and Resources, 57*(20), 6315–6334.

Gao, Y., Lv, H., Hou, Y., Liu, J., & Xu, W. (2019). Real-time modeling and simulation method of digital twin production line. In *Institute of Electrical and Electronics Engineers (IEEE) 8th Joint International Information Technology and Artificial Intelligence Conference*, Chongqing, China (pp. 1639–1642).

Glaessgen, E., & Stargel, D. (2012). The digital twin paradigm for future NASA and U.S. Air Force vehicles. In *Proceedings of the 53rd AIAA/SME/ASCE/AHS/ASC Structures Structural Dynamics and Materials Conference*, 23–26 April. Honolulu, Hawaii. doi:10.2514/6.2012-18

Grieves, M. (2014). *Digital Twin: Manufacturing excellence through virtual factory replication.* Retrieved from https://www.apriso.com

Kabaldin, Y. G., Shatagin, D. A., Anosov, M. S., Kolchin, P. V., & Kuz'mishina, A. M. (2019). CNC machine tools and Digital Twins. *Russian Engineering Research, 39*(8), 637–644.

Kaewunruen, S., Rungskunroch, P., & Welsh, J. (2018). A digital-twin evaluation of net zero energy building for existing buildings. *Sustainability, 11*(1), 159–164.

Kan, C., & Anumba, C. (2019). Digital twins as the next phase of cyber-physical systems in construction. In *Computing in Civil Engineering, Data, Sensing, and Analytics.* Reston, VA: American Society of Civil Engineers.

Lamb, K. (2019). *Principle-based digital twins: A scoping review.* University of Cambridge Repository. https://doi.org/10.17863/CAM.47094

Okeagu, F. N., & Mgbemena, C. E. (2020). A system review of digital twin systems for improved predictive maintenance of equipment in smart factories. *International Journal of Industrial and Production Engineering (IJIPE), 1*(1), 1–8.

Oracle. (2019). *Oracle R Advanced Analytics for Hadoop (ORAAH release 2.8.0).* Retrieved from https;//www.oracle.com

Ramu, S. P., Boopalan, P., Pham, Q., Maddikunta, P. K., Huynh-The, T., Alazab, M., . . . Gadekallu, T. R. (2022). Federated learning enabled digital twins for smart cities: Concepts, recent advances, and future directions. *Sustainable Cities and Society, 79*(2), 103663. doi:10.1016/j.scs.2021.103663

Rosen, R., Wichert, G., Lo, G., & Bettenhausen, K. D. (2015). About the importance of autonomy and digital twins for the future of manufacturing. *International Federation of Automatic Control (IFAC)-Papers Online, 48*(3), 567–572.

Schleich, B., Anwer, N., Mathieu, L., & Wartzack, S. (2017). Shaping the digital twin for design and production engineering. *CIRP Annals – Manufacturing Technology, 66*(1), 1–10.

Talkhestani, B. A., Jung, T., LindemannSahlab, B. N., Jazdi, N., Schloegl, W., & Weyrich, M. (2019). An architecture of an intelligent digital twin in a cyber-physical production system. *Automatisierungstechnik, 67*(9), 762–782.

Tao, F., Qi, Q., Wang, L., & Nee, A. Y. (2019). Digital twins and cyber-physical systems toward smart manufacturing and Industry 4.0: Correlation and comparison. *Engineering, 5*(4), 653–661.

Tao, F., Sui, F., Liu, A., Qi, Q., Zhang, M., Song, B., . . . Andrew, Y. (2019). Digital twin-driven product design framework. *International Journal of Production Research, 57*(12), 3935–3953.

Tharma, R., Winter, R., & Eigner, M. (2019). An approach for the implementation of Digital Twin in the automotive wiring harness field. *International Journal of Production Research, 6*(11), 3023–3032.

Vatn, J. (2018). *Industry 4.0 and real-time synchronization of operation and maintenance: Safety and reliability safe societies in a changing world* (1st ed.). Retrieved from https://www.taylorfrancis.com

Wagner, R., Schleich, B., Haefner, B., Kuhnle, A., Wartzack, S., & Lanza, G. (2019). Challenges and potentials of digital twins and Industry 4.0 in product design and production for high performance products. *Procedia CIRP, 84*(2), 88–93. doi:10.1016/j.procir.2019.04.219

Wang, L., Deng, T., ShenHu, Z. J. M. H., & Qi, Y. (2022). Digital twin-driven smart supply chain. *Frontier of Engineering and Management*, *9*(1), 56–70. doi:10.1007/s42524-021-0186-9

Wang, J., Ye, L., Gao, R. X., Li, C., & Zhang, L. (2019). Digital twins for rotating machinery fault diagnosis in smart manufacturing. *International Journal of Production Research*, *57*(12), 3920–3934. doi:10.1080/00207543.2018.1552032

Wu, P., Qi, M., Gao, L., Zou, W., Miao, Q., & Liu, L. (2019). Research on the virtual reality synchronization of workshop Digital Twin. In *Institute of Electrical and Electronics Engineers (IEEE) 8th Joint International Information Technology and Artificial Intelligence Conference (ITAIC)*, Chongqing, China (pp. 875–879). doi: 10.1109/ITAIC.2019.8785552

Xie, X., Lu, Q., Parlikad, A. K., & Schooling, J. M. (2020). Digital Twin enabled asset anomaly detection for building facility management. *IFAC-PapersOnLine*, *53*(3), 380–385.

Zhang, H., Zhang, G., & Yan, Q. (2019). Digital twin-driven cyber-physical production system towards smart shop-floor. *Journal of Ambient Intelligence and Humanized Computing*, *10*(1), 4439–4453. doi:10.1007/s12652-018-1125-4

List of Books by the Authors

(1) Ikuabe M, Aigbavboa CO, Anumba CJ and **Oke AE** (2023). *A Roadmap for the Uptake of Cyber-Physical Systems for Facilities Management*, London: Routledge Taylor and Francis. 144 Pages. ISBN10: 1032446668; ISBN13: 9781003376262; https://doi.org/10.1201/9781003376262

(2) **Oke AE** (2022). *Measures of Sustainable Construction Projects Performance*, Bingley: Emerald Publishing Limited. 163 pages. ISBN: 9781803829982; eISBN 978-1-80382-997-5; https://doi.org/10.1108/9781803829975

(3) Osunsanmi TO, Aigbavboa CO, Thwala WD and **Oke AE** (2022). *Construction Supply Chain Management in the Fourth Industrial Revolution Era*, Bingley: Emerald Publishing Limited. 337 pages. ISBN: 978-1-80382-160-3 (Print); 978-1-80382-159-7 (Online); 978-1-80382-161-0 (Epub); https://doi.org/10.1108/9781803821597

(4) **Oke AE, Stephen SS,** Aigbavboa CO, Ogunsemi DR and Aje IO (2022). *Smart Cities: A Panacea for Sustainable Development*, Bingley: Emerald Publishing Limited. 193 pages. ISBN: 978-1-80382-456-7 (Print); ISBN: 978-1-80382-455-0 (E-ISBN); ISBN: 978-1-80382-457-4 (Epub); https://doi.org/10.1108/9781803824550

(5) **Oke AE, Stephen SS** and Aigbavboa CO (2022). *Value Management Implementation in Construction – A Global View*, Bingley: Emerald Publishing Limited. 273 pages. ISBN: 978-1-80262-408-3 (Print); ISBN: 978-1-80262-407-6 (Online); ISBN: 978-1-80262-409-0 (Epub); https://doi.org/10.1108/9781802624076

(6) **Oke AE, Stephen SS**, Aigbavboa CO and Thwala WD (2021). *Sustainable Construction in the Era of the Fourth Industrial Revolution*, Bingley: Routledge Taylor and Francis. 184 Pages. ISBN-13: 9781032012155; ISBN-10: 1032012153; https://doi.org/10.1201_9781003179849

(7) Aghimien DO, Aigbavboa CO, **Oke AE** and Thwala WD (2021). *Construction Digitalisation: A Capability Maturity Model for Construction Organisations*, Bingley: Routledge Taylor and Francis. 258 pages. ISBN 9780367758547; ISBN 9781003164654 (eBook); https://doi.org/10.1201/9781003164654

(8) **Oke AE** and Aigbavboa CO (2017). *Sustainable Value Management for Construction Projects*, Switzerland: Springer International Publishing. 201 pages. ISBN 978-3-319-54150-1; ISBN 978-3-319-54151-8 (eBook); https://doi.org/10.1007/978-3-319-54151-8

(9) Ogunsemi DR, Awodele OA and **Oke AE** (2015). *Confluence of Research, Theory and Practice in Quantity Surveying Profession for a Sustainable Built Environment,* Proceeding of the 2nd Nigerian Institute of Quantity Surveyors Research Conference (NIQS ReCon2). ISBN: 978-978-949-128-5

Index